In the Sweet By and By

The Winsome Ways of Miz Eudora Rumph

Volume One

To our special "Mom" with love, "Blessings of fun and laughter for a Merry Christmas! Miz Eudora & Catherine Ritch Guess November 9, 2007

BOOKS BY
CATHERINE RITCH GUESS

EAGLES WINGS TRILOGY
Love Lifted Me
Higher Ground

SHOOTING STAR SERIES
In the Bleak Midwinter
A Song in the Air

SANDMAN SERIES
Old Rugged Cross
Let Us Break Bread Together
Victory in Jesus

- - - - -

In the Garden
Church in the Wildwood
For the Beauty of the Earth
Tis So Sweet
Be Still, My Soul
The Friendly Beasts

CHILDREN'S BOOKS
Kipper Finds a Home
Rudy the Red Pig (Rudy el Puerco Rojo)
Rudy and the Magic Sleigh

MUSICAL CDS
Musical Sculptures
This Is My Song

In the Sweet By and By

The Winsome Ways of Miz Eudora Rumph

Volume One

CATHERINE RITCH GUESS

CRM BOOKS

Publishing Hope for Today's Society

Inspirational Books~CDs~Children's Books

CRM BOOKS, PO Box 2124, Hendersonville, NC 28793

Visit our Web site at www.ciridmus.com

Printed in the United States of America
ISBN (10 digit): 1-933341-20-3
ISBN (13 digit): 9781933341200
LCCN: 9781933341200

In Memory of
Edith Edna Cunningham Howard

My maternal grandmother,
a faithful and feisty mountain woman
in her own right,
born and bred
in Bryson City, North Carolina
where her grandfather was the first
Superintendent of Schools for Swain County

Were she still alive,
she would surely be best friends
with Miz Eudora Rumph

AND

To fun-loving, frivolous
Red Hatters everywhere!

A Special Thanks

I would be greatly remissed if I didn't give a word of special thanks to some wonderful and extraordinary individuals for their help and inspiration in the creation of "The Winsome Ways of Miz Eudora Rumph."

The first and foremost goes to Mark Barden, for not only creating John G. and Mabel T. Jarvis (and writing John G.'s obituary), but for introducing me to Smackass Gap. Also, for being Miz Eudora's personal costume designer and making the purple fur coat I envisioned. You have been most instrumental in the creation of this entire six book series. Without your invaluable imagination and encouragement, there would be no "Winsome Ways of Miz Eudora Rumph." Keep the phone calls and stories coming!

And to Mark's wife, Barbara, and their son, Chris, thanks for not only enduring our combined creative juices, but adding stories and fuel to the flame! Most of all, thanks for being my "adopted" family!

Oh, and Mark, I know why I'm an only child. Had I had a brother, he'd have been just like you and my sweet little mother could not have stood both of us!

To Dot Morrison, of New Bern, NC, whose energy, spark and wit inspired the character of Hattie Crow. May we share many more fun beach trips and treasured times together!

To my other "beach sisters" - Rita Huffman, Marlene Burris, Mary Beth Pugh, Peggy Phelps and Vickie White - thanks for making Hattie come to life on the page, and for enduring all the writing deadlines, phone calls and gathering of "Angel" shells for Rudy's Great Gulf Adventures on our "vacation." Here's to many more excursions!

To my precious mother and sounding board, Corene Howard Ritch, who not only didn't disown me when she read the unedited *In the Sweet By and By*, but now keeps her eyes and ears open for new Miz Eudora adventures. Buckle your seatbelt, for you're on the next ride!

To my poor father, who had to see his first glimpse of Miz Eudora while recovering from a massive heart attack and quadruple bypass surgery. Or perhaps I should acknowledge the surgeon for making sure he didn't suffer another one!

To Josh and Jamie, thanks for not only enduring me, and my wild characters, but for making appearances with us. ***You ARE my sunshine!*** And kudos to all of your friends, who have been told on countless occasions, "Do not encourage our mother!"

And most especially, Mama, Daddy, Josh and Jamie, thanks for always allowing me to be like Miz Eudora, exactly who and what I am, and still loving me.

To each and every one of you, I love you and cherish your friendship more than words can tell.

ACKNOWLEDGMENTS

To Pastor Randy Manser, and wife Linda, whose love of Clay County, and whose time, energy, guided tours, hospitality and use of their "Sweet By and By" cottage were most instrumental in the writing of this series

To Reverend Jacob Kyker, "the big guy under the 'Big Guy,'" who was the inspiration for Preacher Jake's compassion and love of his congregation

To these individuals, each of who served as a plethora of information of a time and place gone by in the enchanted land of Smackass Gap and Clay County, and whose time and stories have provided many "precious memories" for the next volume of "The Winsome Ways of Miz Eudora Rumph": Rob Tiger, owner of Tiger's Chinquapin on the Square; Tommy Hooper, owner of Hayesville Family Restaurant, called "The Fam" or "HFR" (pronounced heifer) by many locals; Clay and Judy Logan, owners of Clay's Corner in beautiful downtown Brasstown, North Carolina, "O'Possum Capital of the South"; Dr. Daniel F. Stroup, Murphy, North Carolina, for filling me in on the Brasstown Brigade; Mary Fonda, the librarian in Hayesville, whose help and insight far exceeded her line of duty; Carl Moore, lifetime resident and historian of Clay County; Molly, of the Clay County Historical and Arts Council; Sergeant Keith H. Mills, U. S. Tennessee Valley Authority Police, Appalachian Sector; and Gladys Jarrett for sharing her lifelong insight into the area

To Jim and Sue Trollinger, Miz Eudora's "special friends," for all their prayers, encouragement and forebearance in birthing this book, not to mention many other things!

To Ella Mae Weems, a Red Hatter from d'Iberville, Mississippi, for her fun spirit and saintly attitude about church music. Once a clown, she still delights many with her angelic face and smile.

To Peggy Donald, Red Hat Nanny, red hat maker extraordinaire whose hats are as glamorous as she is.

To Donna Outen Jenkins, Queen Angelbreeze, a childhood acquaintance who shared the piano bench with me during recital duets. It's been a blessing to cross paths again after too many years. How fun it was to join your Red Hat chapter of Hot G.R.I.T.S. and Red Hats (now Red Hat Sisters in Christ), only to find that I had fond memories of most of your members from childhood and adolescent years.

To Barbara Brooks Taylor, childhood friend and school classmate. Our grandmothers, who were best friends, lived across the road from each other and shared many afternoon front porch chats. Here's to soon sharing our own front porch chats from across that same road, in our red and purple! And thanks for bringing all of our childhood friends together again for a taste of "home."

And, lastly, to all of my dear readers who have sent delightful "Miz Eudora stories" and have spurned me on during the process of introducing Miz Eudora Rumph to the world.

A Note from Catherine

You are about to embark on a fantastic journey. Hopefully, it is a journey that will continue each day of your life as you look for the bright spots in everyday living. May it inspire you to find humor in the simplest things in life, and gloss with ease over life's most trying moments – all with the unadorned, pure faith of a child. Most of all, may it release you from taking yourself too seriously and give you the ability and self-confidence to laugh at yourself and the world around you, finding great pleasure in *all* that surrounds you.

My three wishes for each reader of *In the Sweet By and By* are that you begin to recognize and relish those "Miz Eudora" moments, that you capture a "Miz Eudora" moment each day of your life, *and* you use those "Miz Eudora" moments to light up the world of others around you!

Sit down, take a relaxing breath, kick your feet up, and take a big swig of iced tea – sweetened or unsweetened, as your locale fancies – as you prepare for one of the most joyous of "joy rides" in your life. Oh, and no need to buckle up!

Blessed travels,
CR?

In the Sweet
By and By

PROLOGUE

I FIRST MET Mrs. Eudora Rumph on a warm summer's afternoon. The kind of afternoon that you quickly learn, in the far western reaches of the North Carolina mountains, is magical. Magical for it mysteriously and miraculously appears from the hazy, almost translucent fog that lies low to the ground until about mid-morning, followed by the still heavy dew on the grass. And then comes that moment, that magical moment like something out of a story from Camelot, when suddenly everything is unbelievably clear and brilliant. So much so that it looks like the result of a masterful painter's brush, creating a richly vibrant landscape, rather than a view out the window into one's front yard. Especially when one's front yard has previously been downtown skyscrapers, too-heavily-traveled thoroughfares and miles and miles of continuous shopping malls.

Following my husband Leon's death, I moved to a place that I had visited with him, during a weekend years before, when he was still in a practicing career as a counselor. It was the setting of a retreat he was leading, and it seemed we'd driven far enough to fall off the other side of the continent, when magically-as magically as that summer afternoon when I first met "Miz Eudora"- we happened upon the most ethereal place I'd ever seen. "Heavenly" did not begin to do the place justice. And it was indeed heaven on earth, for one of God's truest saints–I quickly learned after my move there–was Eudora Rumph, known to folks all over Clay County simply as "Miz Eudora."

I shouldn't actually say we "happened upon." For since that time, I've come to learn there was no happenchance involved at all. It was strictly a meant-to-be experience that we crossed an invisible line where a sign welcomed us to Clay County and we found ourselves at the bottom of Chunky Gal Mountain.

I shall never forget that afternoon of discovery with my husband. The sign announcing "Chunky Gal Mountain" brought such a rise out of both Leon and me that all we could think about was that childhood game of *Candyland* and that folksong about the *Big Rock Candy Mountain.*

My husband glanced at me, after recovering from his bout of laughter, and said, "Sadie, the only thing missing is six white horses coming round the mountain." He immediately began to sing, a bit off-key, that verse of *She'll Be Coming Round the Mountain*.

Looking back on that afternoon with Leon, I do believe that if we'd sat at that spot for a few minutes, Miz Eudora might have truly appeared, "coming round the mountain," with those six white horses. *Or maybe mules*. And there's no doubt in my mind that "we'd have all had chicken and dumplings" once she made that turn around the mountain.

I'm also sure it was *not* a part of the happenchance - excuse me, "meant to be" - experience that we meet Miz Eudora on that afternoon. That was to come later. Much later. After the passing of my husband, Leon Callaway.

But, *had* she come around Chunky Gal Mountain that afternoon, it would have greatly behooved us to "all go out to meet her" and we'd have surely been "singing 'Hallelujah' when she come."

Oh well, I could go on all day about this wonderful woman, the epitome of a generation of mountain women gone by, but I think you'd enjoy her much more if you met her yourself. So without further adieu, allow me to take you to Smackass Gap, the small community at the bottom of Chunky Gal Mountain, and introduce you to Mrs. Eudora Rumph, whom you'll soon come to learn as "Miz Eudora."

Oh, and so you can fully grasp the full flavor of Miz Eudora and Smackass Gap, I'll do my best to tell the story using her vernacular.

Best wishes,
Sadie Callaway

GLOSSARY OF
MIZ EUDORA'S SPEECH HABITS

afraid – a'feared
because – 'cause
can't – cain't
could of – could'a
going to – gonna
heard - heared
I came to - I come to
ing – in'
seen – see'd
sure – shore
that's going to – what's gonna
was – wuz
wasn't – wadn't
we were – we was
would of – would'a
you all - ya'll

You get the picture!

ONE

In the Sweet By and By

THE SCENE WAS set for a remarkably gorgeous early fall day as I walked across the street - oh, excuse me, "road"; we don't have streets here in the mountains of "way-far western" North Carolina. Anyway, as I was saying, the sky was perfect. There was not a cloud in it and its blue color was so vibrant and clear that it seemed one could see forever. Not a native of the state, I saw why some Carolinians challenged, "If God is not a Tarheel fan, then why is the sky Carolina blue?" Looking at that blue sky now, I concluded that to the dismay of NC State, Duke and Wake Forest fans, they would have a difficult time debating that issue.

There had been a light mist earlier that morning, the kind of dewfall that kisses the earth just enough to make everything come alive. "Stand up and take notice," they say here in Clay County. Pretty much like young love in springtime and that hint of a first kiss. There was also just enough residue of the moisture left on the tips of leaves and blades of grass to wrap a veil of shimmer on their edges.

Birds seemed to sense the changing season, too, for their songs were akin to a rescinding crescendo of "Glorias" at the end of a great choral work. They seemed to be calling antiphonally from one mountainside to the other, as if to say "goodbye until next spring" or "see you in a warmer climate." The richness of their musical dialogue was heightened by the faintest smell of drying hay at the neighboring farms, further eluding to the epilogue of a pastorale.

The air was tinged with a crispness that reached just deep enough into the soul to remind one that complacency with this scenery and aura was not an option. It wasn't yet time for a jacket, at least for the local mountaineers, but in short sleeves, one did not take time to "lollygag around."

It is a picture perfect day, all right, all of my senses agreed as I quickly swept past the mailbox of Horace and Eudora Rumph on foot that morning. In the wake of those glorious surroundings, it was hard to imagine that anything bad could happen to ruin such a faultless start of a day. My only thought of sadness was that Leon was not walking beside me, holding my hand, to also enjoy it.

"Yes," I definitely decided and softly muttered, "there's nothing in the world that can take away from the beauty of this day." My words, offered to the heavens as a personal soliloquy to Leon and a thanks to the day's Maker, ended as I reached the massive flower garden that greeted visitors at the front of the Rumph home.

I would preferred to have been back on my own side of the road planting mums and digging my hands in the rich, fertile black soil of those mountains, but the task at hand seemed the "neighborly thing to do" for the moment. The mums and soil would be there an hour later. Given the reason for the visit to the home of Miz Eudora Rumph, I was sure that a few minutes would suffice and I would be back tending to my own flower garden in no time.

I had heard, through the proverbial grapevine along which all community news travels in that section of the country, that her husband Horace "was ailing" so I "fixed up" a basket of food and tried to return the down-home hospitality that Miz Eudora had extended to me upon my move to Smackass Gap a few months prior. Lord only knows why I had the nerve to take food to the best cook in all of Clay County, North Carolina.

Well, actually I do know why I had the nerve. That little voice that creeps into one's head from time to time told me I should. At the time I started across the street – *road!* - with the picnic basket in tow, I had no idea for the reason of that little voice at that particular moment earlier that morning. It only took a couple of minutes, as long as it took me to take three steps inside the Rumph home, to discover the purpose of the little voice. The neighborly thing to do turned out to be much more than that.

"Sadie!" I heard Miz Eudora yell as I tapped lightly on the screen door and then opened it, its aged creaking serving as a familiar Clay County doorbell. There was a slight edge of panic, a sort of urgency not at all customary for this epitome of a mountain woman, in her voice. "Come on back here." What, for her, would normally have been spoken as a natural hard-edged command was delivered more as a plea. Not only a plea, but also one tinged with shaky uncertainty.

I sat the picnic basket down on the kitchen table, covered in a green-and-white checked tablecloth and bearing two freshly-baked apple pies, and headed toward the back corner of the house from whence the voice had come. "I came over to check on…,"

My words broke off as I saw the reason for Miz Eudora's state of uncertainty. Horace lay on the bed, appearing to be in a calm and peaceful sleep, but with no sign of breathing. With knees buckling and a suddenly nauseous stomach, I glanced back at her, noting her disheveled appearance and the flour still on her apron. That, in itself, gave indication that she was not her usual tower of strength.

When I finally caught my own breath and felt the weakening of my knees subside, I hesitantly asked, "How…long…has he…been like this?" I noticed that my own voice sounded like the shaky one I'd heard from her only seconds earlier.

"I was coming back to check on him," she explained. "He always comes straight to the kitchen for a piece of warm pie and a glass of milk just about the time the fruit filling cools enough to eat. 'Specially when he'd just brought in a basket of fresh Winesap apples earlier in the morning, He laid down this morning after bringing in the apples and the fall beans and said he was going to rest up a spell. When the pies was ready, I called him a couple of times and got no answer, so I decided to come back here and check on him. It seems I'd no

more than walked in the doorway here when I heard
you at the door. But then again, it could of been a
few minutes. I was just thinking I'd better trot across
the road to see if you'd call the sheriff's office."

"I'll run home and call right now," I offered,
still in shock, "but do you think I should call the
ambulance?"

"What for? They ain't into raising the dead
'round these here parts," she answered.

I knew she was completely serious, and had
it been under any other circumstance, I'd have found
her reply quite humorous. But then, those logical
uncanny remarks were what made this broken mold
of a mountain woman "Miz Eudora."

"Very well, then," I called behind me as I
took off out the front door. "I'll notify the sheriff's
office."

Halfway across the road, it dawned on me
that I hadn't even told the poor old woman that I
was sorry. *Oh well,* I thought as I continued to sprint
toward my own front door and the telephone just
beyond, *I can do that after I call the sheriff's
office. I'm sure she'll understand.*

I thought of the ambiguity in her voice from
when she'd called out to me. *On second thought,
I don't even think she noticed.* My mind raced
back to my own situation of Leon's death several

months back. *I understand the feeling*, I recalled.

As soon as I hung up from the sheriff's office, I called Miz Eudora's pastor. "Preacher Jake," she called him. I figured that between those two fine upstanding pillars of the community, they could contact anyone else who might need to be called in. I felt it my "bounden duty" to rush back to console my neighbor, the same one whose tongue-in-cheek comments had consoled me since the loss of my Leon.

Or, I reasoned, *at least since my move to the hidden gem of Clay County – Smackass Gap*.

IT WAS SHERIFF Albert Bonner who arrived first. I was pleased to see that this was a job that called for the head honcho and not one of the deputies. He took care of business and commenced to call the coroner and the Smiley Funeral Parlor from his radio as soon as he was content that no foul play had been committed. I'm sure he knew that before his arrival, but it was simply a matter of course.

His well-groomed, towering figure was a stark contrast to the short frame, and hunched-over shoulders of grief, on this woman whose husband was now the "dearly departed." I'd never seen the sheriff before, but my immediate reaction was that he had once been the football captain at Hayesville High School. I watched as he placed his large right palm on her shoulder.

Good tactic, I thought. *Those football hands, made for receiving any pass he's thrown, appear to be full of comfort.* I concluded that my judgment was correct when I saw Miz Eudora's shoulders straighten a bit, a sign of her returning strength.

"How are we doing today, Miz Eudora?" Sheriff Bonner asked.

How are we doing today? I heard my subconscious repeating, unable to believe his sudden fumble. *Well, one of us is dead, and one of us is standing here, shoulders hunched, hair a mess, appearance wrecked and has just lost our life's mate of decades. And you want to know how we're doing?*

There would be no touchdown for this man, and I was in no mood for replays, even though his question continued to ring in my ears. I'm sure his words were meant to serve as a cordial greeting, but he'd obviously had no training in the consolation department. *Maybe he'd better check into the Yellow Jackets' coaching job at the high school and get back to the field!*

"How do you *think* we're doing?" I wanted

to scream, but I knew better. That was Miz Eudora's job. Had this been any other day, I'm sure those would have been the very words out of her mouth, but today, she was in no shape to give anyone "what for" or "down the country."

"Miz Eudora," I heard softly from behind me as the preacher walked into the room where Horace still lay. In his voice floated the soothing tranquility of a warm summer's breeze, a welcome resolve to the approaching fall days that would be accompanied by evenings with light frost.

Touchdown! My mind envisioned the image of Jesus with hands raised skyward, a statue well known from Indiana's Notre Dame campus and often referred to as "Touchdown Jesus." Now I understood a whole new meaning of that statue, for here was a man, *a Godly man*, who knew not only how to catch the ball, but run it the length of the field. *He scores in the consolation department!*

"I come as quick as I could." His choice of words told me that he'd found a common ground with his church members. His choice of timing told me that "he'd come," right on cue, to save the day.

Preacher Jake Turner, a man in his early forties, had been the pastor of First Church, Smackass, since his late twenties. I'd heard Miz Eudora speak of him in nearly every conversation

I'd had with her. From her kind comments - that is, as kind as they come from Miz Eudora - it was obvious that she held this man in high regard. I was sure it wasn't because of his position as a "man of the cloth," for she was the kind of woman who could see straight through an imposter.

And one whose wrath would put to shame any insincere acts of an imposter, I determined, chuckling aloud at the image of her, even at age eighty-three, putting a "defrocked" minister on his trail.

I now ventured to watch as Preacher Jake laid a caring hand on his parishioner's other shoulder, noting that his mannerisms truly did speak of a genuine concern for the bereaved rather than the necessary one attached to his ministerial robe – a robe which I doubted came with his call to this laidback mountain area.

He turned to me, rightfully assuming that since I was the only one there, I'd made the contact. "Thank you for calling."

I nodded silently, not wishing to break his consolation to the newly claimed widow. I'm not too sure that the silence didn't stem rather from not knowing what to say. But it seemed to be the right thing for the moment, whatever reason. I merely lingered in the corner of the bedroom, hoping my presence was enough to allow Miz Eudora to sense my sorrow for her situation. A part of me was, in reality, surprised that I was capable of taking on this role. After all, the entire scenario rang all too familiar to what I had experienced myself less than a year before.

As I listened to the friendly exchange between the sheriff and the preacher, with Miz Eudora adding a comment from time to time, I watched her and thought of the many lessons she had taught me in the few months I'd known her. I was sure that in the somberness of this moment, there was yet another monumental lesson to be learned. How little did I know that this lesson would serve as the opening chapter of an entire textbook of life's greatest lessons. Not only for me, but also for many other women. And even for some men before it would all be said and done. Invaluable lessons that I would later term *The Winsome Ways of Miz Eudora Rumph*.

I answered a knock at the door. A man standing there, dressed in a black suit with a white starched shirt, alerted me that the funeral home attendant had come for the body. I opened the door, nodding genially at the man as I directed him to Horace's bedroom. A second man, dressed just the same except for a different name on his plastic

Smiley Funeral Parlor nametag, followed close behind.

Both men offered a friendly, yet somber, greeting to the preacher and the sheriff. It was obvious that, over the years, they had become oblivious to the awkwardness of this type of situation, but were still very much sympathetic to the bereaving widow.

I moved to the kitchen and helped myself to a small plate of the food I'd brought over. *It isn't like Indian-giving*, I thought defensively as I felt a pang of guilt ripple through my body. *Horace has no use for it now, and I'd be embarrassed for Miz Eudora to taste my cooking*.

Not that my cooking was bad. It was just that everyone's cooking placed far down the line when compared to hers. She must have had every blue ribbon for every domestic category there was from the annual county fair hanging from her back screened porch – the area where she'd made all those awards happen. I'd never stayed long enough to see how far back they dated, but a quick glance told you that she was not one to be reckoned with in the kitchen area, not to mention gardening and making things with her hands.

"If we could all form a circle 'round Brother Horace's bed and join hands, I'll commence to blessing Horace's death and asking God to watch over Miz Eudora here."

Preacher Jake's voice beckoned me to turn my attention from my stomach to the situation at hand. I felt more like I was circling up around the campfire of a John Wayne western, ready to sing a few songs to a harmonica accompaniment before retiring for the evening, rather than praying over a corpse. Of all the things I'd ever envisioned myself doing in my lifetime, this was not one of them.

At the conclusion of the prayer, Preacher Jake pulled up a chair for Miz Eudora and then one for himself. The rest of us paid them no attention as he placed a hand over hers and offered a few more comforting words. He then motioned for one of the funeral home attendants to move closer as he asked a couple of questions regarding how she wished the service to be handled.

"I reckon I'm a' gonna to have to haul out that blamed old cedar chest and find my black wool dress," she bellowed across the room, causing all the other heads to veer toward her. "It would have been decent of Horace to done that for me a'fore his passing, but then I reckon he wasn't a'figuring on crossing the Jordan this morning."

I caught a muffled snicker from Sheriff Bonner. I'd already had to muffle a few of my own snickers that morning, the least of which was the thought that the Smiley Funeral Home's slogan should have been, "We'll be the last ones to put a smile on your face." As that again ran through my mind, I lowered my head and appeared to wipe my eyes, hoping they wouldn't notice my cover-up.

There was really no need to try to hide my smirk, though, for at that moment Miz Eudora blurted, "Humph! I'll bet'cha anything that wool dress is full of moth holes. Horace could of had the consideration to left in the spring. I've got lots of flowery dresses made from those old flour sacks we used to use. Why, you couldn't wear one of those things out if you wanted to."

With that statement, even the Smiley boys lost the battle of trying to keep their toothy grins inaudible, as their faces now resembled the yellow smiley faces on their plastic name badges.

"Oh, no, Miz Eudora," Preacher Jake replied as he quickly broke into the conversation, trying to save the room from a full-blown outburst of laughter. "You don't need to worry about moth holes, or even that black wool dress. This is going to be a celebration of Mr. Horace's life." His statement, emphasizing the word "celebration," followed the modern-day philosophy that had replaced the morbid manner of thinking about death in the way of days gone by. I'd heard the same uplifting comments of encouragement during the time of Leon's passing.

"Celebration?" squawked Miz Eudora. "Why, Preacher Jake, I didn't know everybody was so glad Horace died!"

That's how it was that I came to learn the power of my own self-will, for I did not roll in the floor with a belly laugh, even though Sheriff Bonner and one of the Smiley boys were not as successful as I.

That's also how it was that I came to learn there is life after death, for from that day forward I watched Miz Eudora Rumph blossom into the fully beautiful creature that God intended her to be. Just as a delicate lily whose petals open wide to see the world from a hearty, closed-up bloom – lovely in itself, but ready to burst forth at the seams in celebration of life.

And boy, oh boy, did she ever burst forth in celebration of life...in the sweet by and by!

TWO

I'll Be Saving You a Place

IN THE FIVE minutes it took me to walk from that bedroom back to the front steps of my house, I might as well have been in a full-length picture show. Every memory of the past eleven months passed right before my eyes, just as vividly as if they had been aboard an old pick-up truck passing by on the road, loaded down with fresh vegetables on its way to the local roadside market of Smackass Gap.

I took a seat in the rocker, the same one that had been the favorite of Leon before his passing, on the front porch. Had it not been for my beloved Leon, I would have never met Miz Eudora. *And*, I realized as I gazed across the road and up the mountain that led to her home, *I would have missed out on the best part of my life.*

Not to say that my life with Leon was not

good. It was truly like a storybook marriage in many ways. In many ways except for the fact that I'd borne him no children. I'd had no offspring to keep me company in my old age, a fact that I wrongly carried as a burden for many years.

But, truth be known, in all those years, I had no inkling that the best was yet to come. I guess "the good Lord," as Miz Eudora was fond of calling Him, knew that she was going to be better company and more entertaining than a host of children and grandchildren could have ever been. After the goings on of the morning, I guess her good Lord also knew that she was going to need a widowed neighbor in her years to come, and thus I lived here, across the "road" so that we could each have someone near and dear.

Thinking back through the minutes since I had left this porch earlier with basket of food in hand, I didn't know which batch of emotions to unleash first. My body was whirling with everything from raucous laughter to dire sympathy to warm arms of a husband who was now gone. My emotions took on a life of their own, seeming to know the order of which they should take their turns. As Leon's face mentally hung in the air between the massive oak branches, I knew what was to come first. I laid my head back against the padded cushion on the chair, closed my eyes and allowed that visual image of his face to frame the rest of my thought process as the gentle front-and-back sway of the rocker lulled my whole being into a peaceful stage for life's theater.

After Leon's sudden death, I was so overcome by grief that I could hardly bear it. During the course of our marriage, the fact that we never had children eventually developed into a point of blessed bliss and happiness, for we had the kind of relationship that perfected with age. I was never sure if that was because Leon was a counselor who specialized in working with couples or because we were so right for each other.

But for whatever reason it *was*, it was *all wrong* after the moment of his passing. I then achingly longed for children that would remind me of Leon, who would possess any of his features, and especially his personality. All I got, though, were long, lonely nights that felt like the worst nightmares of my life. They then grew to overshadow my every waking moment until I thought I would nearly go insane.

One day, Loretta Branton, Leon's secretary of many years came over to visit me. "Sadie, you've absolutely *got* to get a handle on yourself. This is the kind of situation that your husband helped people through his entire career. He, of all people, would not want to see you mourning his loss so greatly. You have got to get on with life. I can hear him saying those same words myself."

The only problem was, I could hear him saying them, too. I'd heard him come home from his office on numerous occasions, never divulging any personal information about a case, but from time to time making a generalization about the people who frequented his office.

"'That woman's simply got to get a grip on her life and move forward. Her husband might have died, but she certainly didn't. It's doing no one any good for her to sit and mourn so day in and day out.'" Even that mere thought of the memory of Leon's words sent me into an emotional spiral that felt as if there was no bottom.

"What do you suggest I do?" I asked Loretta, barely able to put the few words together in my anguish.

"I've heard Leon speak of a place up near Hayesville, North Carolina," she answered without hesitation. "You know the one. It's where he went to teach a three-day seminar at the Hinton Rural Life Center that time." Loretta gave a reminiscent smile. "I distinctly remember it because he'd told you he was taking you with him to some enchanted mountain hideaway for a few days. Only thing when the brochure arrived, he feared his 'hideawa, was instead some God-forsaken hole-in-the-wall. He dreaded telling you so much that he requested the other two days of that week off in hopes that the two of you could visit the Grove Park Inn, or someplace in Asheville, to make up for the disappointment he was sure you'd face. Then, after the retreat when Leon came back to the office, he gloated with delightful tales of how you two never left that area the entire week."

Loretta paused to check for any glimmer of recollection in my face, which she readily found. "Anyway, he occasionally mentioned that the two of you had considered retiring there someday. Why don't you give that some thought?"

"I couldn't possibly go there without him," I slowly admitted. "I'd never be able to get him out of my memory."

"That's the whole point, Sadie," she said. "You're not supposed to go there without him any more than you're supposed to get him out of your memory. He'll be right there with you. It's his memory that will give you the courage to move on and find a new beginning. You go there, you fondly recall all the good times you shared, both there and other places, and you make new friends and continue o live a happy and beautiful life."

I caught the look of anticipation on Loretta's face as she paused to see if her words were seeping in and, more than that, making any hint of difference in my attitude.

As difficult as it was, I managed a half smile as I muttered, "You're right. I know you are. He was right, too. But it's so hard," I whined, returning to my pity party tone.

"Aren't the things in life that are most worthwhile the ones that take the most effort?" she questioned, so much compassion in her voice that I saw why she'd been a perfect secretary for Leon's counseling practice. "I watched the two of you," she continued. "I worked in the same office as Leon for over twenty years and I saw your marriage grow to the point that it seemed the two of you were nearly inseparable. But that 'happy marriage' didn't come without a price, did it? You can't honestly say that there were never any quarrels, any stand-offs, any moments of friction that didn't cause you to be even stronger in your relationship."

Loretta moved to the fireplace and leaned her elbow across the mantle, a habit of Leon's every time he wanted to push an issue, but felt resistance. She gave a sigh, exactly like that one of Leon's when he was searching to find the right words when I knew that he clearly disagreed with something I'd said or done.

I stared at her, appreciating the fact that she had learned much from Leon over the years and wondering if she had any idea that Leon had spoken "from the grave" through her as she relayed a direly-needed message to me.

It was at that precise moment that I knew what I had to do. It was also the moment that I knew I would not do it alone.

It was *not* the moment, however, that made things easier the next morning when I dialed the telephone number of a realtor that had sold several homes in my downtown neighborhood. My distress must have shown on the morning when the realtor dropped by, for she assured me that many couples were doing the same thing of buying a retirement home or a weekend home.

Her choice of words, "many couples," did not help matters at all. She quickly retraced her steps to further inform me how "many widows or widowers also make that choice to find a new place to move, to get on with their lives in a difficult time, to downsize."

I wanted to throw out, "or rather, as an excuse," but I chose better and opted to take a last stroll down the front cobblestone sidewalk, lined by immaculately manicured rows of shrubbery, while she did her appraisal of my once "happily ever after" home.

As I signed the contract allowing her to list my home, she signed a different paper with the name and number of an agent in western North Carolina who could help me find "the perfect place." I was too embarrassed to tell her the name of "the perfect place" that Leon had once spotted at the bottom of Chunky Gal Mountain. "The perfect place" that was surrounded by "lovely little dots in the road" called Shooting Creek, Bear Paw, Hanging Dog, Peckerwood, Jack Rabbit, Muskrat, Licklog, and not to be left out, Elf.

A ripple of laughter ran through me at the thought of saying "Good-bye" to everyone at the country club followed by the announcement that I was moving to Smackass Gap, North Carolina. Suddenly I felt that, too, was Leon's way of saying to me, "Go out. Live it up. Keep that zest in your life. It isn't over yet." He really *had* spoken to me from the grave.

"Well, now, that wasn't so bad, was it?" the realtor asked when she noticed the jovial expression on my face. "I'm glad to see your laughter. Some people have a bit of a fear that they're signing their life away."

I nodded and said nothing as I imagined Leon finishing his last words of counsel to me with, "And I'll be saving you a place."

That's how it was that I came to move to Smackass Gap, North Carolina.

THREE

Beyond the Shadow of a Doubt

"IT'S A QUIETLY quaint area full of some of the most wonderful people on the face of the earth," lauded the Clay County realtor. "Even in the summer, when the population of Clay County triples from all the folk of the Deep South who head for the hills to beat the summer heat and escape the sticky mugginess and hurricanes. I'm sure you won't be sorry."

I was glad *she* was sure, because in spite of endless spiels of positive reinforcement from all the interested parties – *including Leon* – I still had my doubts.

The house I wound up buying was one that Leon and I had spotted on our visit to Smackass Gap. It sat at the bottom of the hill on the road that led up the mountain to Hinton Rural Life Center, and we'd both immediately fallen in love with it the first time we saw it. I couldn't believe my good fortune when the realtor passed it on the morning she took me to see houses and I saw the "For Sale" sign in the yard. A white wooden, one-story frame house, with deep-green doors, shutters and tin roof, it was built in exactly the style of which you'd imagine an old mountain farmhouse.

The front door opened into a big sitting room on the right and a large bedroom to the left. That was the one I chose to use. You walked straight back through a wide hallway to the kitchen and dining room on the back left of the house, and a smaller bedroom on the back right. All of the rooms were spacious by modern standards and all of them had high ceilings. There was even a canning shed, a room I would use for storage, which extended to the rear of the house past the back porch.

I had the strangest feeling that this house was in someway a gift from Leon. I sensed, beyond the shadow of a doubt, that had he still been alive, this would have been the exact house we'd have chosen for our retirement home. It seemed like a piece of treasure, found at the placed marked with an "X" on the map – the map of Clay County.

Months later, I considered all the many treasures of the area's nature – cascading waterfalls, magnificent mountains, lush greenery, splendiferous arrays of flora and fauna – that had convinced Leon and I that we'd like to retire in western North Carolina, to become recluses from the skyscrapers and hustle-bustle of the world. There was *no* doubt in my mind that the most valuable treasure of all, native to Clay County, was a woman named Eudora Rumph.

I sometimes wondered if Eudora had a middle name, but then, with a name like Eudora Rumph, I was more afraid to ask. So that was one subject I never broached during our afternoon front porch chats, which always included a large glass of freshly squeezed lemonade or brewed iced tea. *Sweetened, of course!*

I'd not paid much attention to the house across the "road" when I moved to the bottom of Chunky Gal Mountain. It was "a fer piece" across the field from me, up an incline and directly behind a row of cottonwood trees, with a seldom-used driveway right beside the road sign that announced the community of Smackass Gap.

That was part of the reason I liked the area so much. There was a peacefulness about not being too close to the neighbors, given I'd lived in downtown Atlanta for much of the time Leon and I had been married. Since they were out of sight, they were also out of mind.

That is, until I heard a knock at the front door of my house on Oak Forest on my third day there.

There stood a short, but robust, woman in a well-worn, flowered cotton dress. Its three-quarter length sleeves gave the purple calico print, which looked as if it belonged on a quilt rather than a body, more of a fall appearance than a spring garb. A warm smile was written all over her elderly, but glowing, face and was accented by eyes of blue, the same color and sparkle as Lake Chatuge just down the road. Her dull gray hair, which I suspected had never been cut, was balled up on the top of her head. As I peered out the screen door at her, I gathered she was definitely a native of the area.

"I didn't come to call," she said in a boisterous voice that I could imagine yodeling over the hillsides. "You're too busy for that right now. My name is Eudora Rumph, and I just wanted to welcome you to the neighborhood with a homemade apple pie. My husband, Horace, picked the apples from our trees back up the mountain behind the house. Living right next to Smackass Branch helps keep the apples producing. You come on over anytime you feel like it after you git settled in and all." She never said bye or anything else as she took off back across the road as quickly and quietly as "she'd come."

That's how it was that I came to meet Miz Eudora Rumph.

OVER THE COMING months, I came to learn that Mrs. Eudora Rumph was a woman of great faith.

She was also a woman of great proportion. So was her husband Horace. Horace Buchanan Rumph. "H'arse," it sounded like when she pronounced it. I never quite understood how one-syllable words like "gap" phonetically sounded like they had at least three syllables, and two-syllable words like "Horace" sounded like they had only one. And that one syllable was always spoken rather pointedly. Not like that rich southern drawl you hear on the east coast of North Carolina, or in the deep reaches of Mississippi, but in a dialect all its own. I'd never heard anyone talk quite like her, and I hope I never shall, for that is a delightfully pleasant asset that suits her to a tee. Unless, that is, I take it up in my elderly years as a resident of "Sa-mac-ka-us Ga-i-up."

The first time I actually "met" and spent any time with Mrs. Rumph was shortly after I'd had to go to the hospital for one of those same-day procedures that every person over fifty dreads.

When I went shopping on the following afternoon, feeling the need for a little compassion and company, I did the neighborly thing of taking her a grocery bag full of necessities, one of which was a roll of paper towels.

"That's a mighty wide roll of toilet paper," she'd commented as she removed it from the bag. "Why, even Horace Rumph's rump isn't that big!"

"Mrs. Rumph," I told her, not sure whether I was more amused or shocked, "that isn't toilet paper. That's to use for spills in the kitchen."

"Why, thank you," she replied politely. "That's mighty nice, but we don't spill ours in the kitchen. We got ourselves a brand new enamel slop jar in the closet." She leaned across the table toward me. "That sounds a little more mannerly than calling it a chamber pot." While I struggled not to laugh, she sat back upright as if that was quite enough of an explanation. "Horace takes it out the back door, not through the kitchen."

That's how it was that I had my first "experience" with Mrs. Eudora Rumph.

Before that afternoon chat was over with, I'd learned that one of her most profound Eudoraisms was, "If we can't laugh at ourselves, who are we going to laugh at?"

From that day on, she was known to me

simply as plain old "Miz Eudora," just like she was to the rest of Chunky Gal Mountain, Bear Paw, Hanging Dog (pronounced Hangin' Dawg), Shooting Creek (pronounced Shootin' Crick)… and Smackass Gap (pronounced just like that).

That's also how I came to learn – *beyond the shadow of a doubt* – that I was where I was meant to be, on the authority of both Leon *and* the Power Beyond.

FOUR

Mules and a Fat Lady

AFTER THAT FIRST "experience" with Miz Eudora, I came to look forward to my daily dose of experiences with her. She, her anecdotes and her funny ways – which were nothing but living and let live, and enjoying every moment of life in its purest and most simplistic form – were what helped me through my period of grieving over my dear Leon.

The realtor was right. I came to realize that I *wasn't* sorry and that living across the road from the Rumph house was the best thing that could have ever happened to me. ***Beyond the shadow of a doubt.***

Our first afternoon chat happened when I went to ask Miz Eudora about how the community of Smackass Gap got its name. I knew there had to be a good story there and I was sure she was just the one to tell it.

"So, Miz Eudora," I began, sipping from the glass of refreshment that was half sweet tea and half lemonade (a concoction I was sure she'd been serving since long before it became known as an Arnold Palmer), "how did Smackass Gap get its name?"

"Well…,"

Already her first word had me intrigued. There was something about the way she spoke that drew you into every syllable. Not to mention the fact that anytime a story began with the word "Well," you knew you were in for a "good 'urn!"

"…It's like this, years ago, they used to mine for corundum over in Elf. The miners used mules to pull the wagons, and when they came to the gap, they'd hit the mules on the rump. That made the mules pull a little harder so they could get the wagons up the rise on the other side."

She took a big swig of tea and rocked back and forth, staring out at the same spot on the side of the mountain that I was to learn she always stared at when she sat on the front porch. I waited for her to finish the rest of the story, but she didn't say "nary" a word.

"You mean that's all there is to it?" I asked, the disappointment showing in my voice. So much so that it sounded more like a plea for a piece of juicy gossip than a question.

She never "missed a lick" with her rocking as she replied, "There was another story once. It had something to do with a fat lady."

Oh, good! I thought, anticipating the colorful story.

Miz Eudora continued to rock and enjoy her tea.

"And?" I prodded, thinking how "the good Lord" must smile on this creature because "dirty laundry" was sure not to be aired where she was concerned.

Her face showed a slight blush as she gave a hushed snicker. "It wasn't very nice, so the one about the mules is the one people 'round here consider authentic."

I saw that was all of the story I was going to get, but at least her telling about it was not a total loss. There was something harmonious in the way she pronounced "authentic." Something that brought a comforting smile to my face.

That's how it was that a beautiful friendship began.

UNTIL THAT AFTERNOON, I'd never paid

much attention to the details of the Rumph property. But as we sat on her front porch, which faced Downings Creek Road and was sided by Smackass Branch, her swigging and me sipping, I saw a kind of beauty that I'd never seen anywhere else. Hers was a picturesque place, so much so that I contemplated about how it belonged on the front of a jigsaw puzzle box. It wasn't a manicured property, but at the same time, it wasn't unkempt. Everything within viewing range was so incredibly natural, like it had never been touched since the time the world was made. I immediately respected her husband, Horace, and the Rumphs before him for the way they had cared for the land. There had been no abuse, for sure, in the way they had grown their crops and lumbered their trees.

I looked intensely at her house, trying to soak in every detail, noting with each one how perfectly it matched her personality. The structure was a good bit larger than mine, but its layout was quite the same. Its kitchen and dining room were larger, plus it had a small area that was comparable to what we, today, would consider a breakfast nook. Old white, asbestos shingles covered it on the outside, and older looking green shingles were on the roof. I imagined that it looked now exactly as it had the day it was completed, minus the natural aging.

Barns of various shapes and sizes dotted the hillsides and dips. The barbed wire fence that ran along the driveway and the road front was probably even the same one that Horace had put up as soon as he'd finished the house, which I highly suspected had been for their wedding. I didn't dare ask how long ago that had been, for I'd heard tales of how early some of those mountain women had "got hitched." Besides, I knew there would be "a'plenty" of other afternoon chats for that.

The afternoon rolled around to early evening at a snail's pace as the cows came right up to the front steps and chewed their cud. Goats feasted on the grass around the porch, keeping it an attractive height. I knew there had to be at least one hog and some chickens, but I had no idea how many other forms of livestock. As I sat there, I realized it was the first time I'd ever sat on the front porch of a farm. Yet, with Miz Eudora rocking beside me, it felt I'd been there all my life.

What mattered most about it, at least in my opinion, was the warmth that exuded from the inside of the house to the outside world. Sure, I could already tell that Miz Eudora could look straight at you and give you "down the country" if she didn't like something about you. But she could also shower you with love in her own, unique style. Her love wasn't something you had to earn; it was simply there, just like her faith. Love and faith, both such complicated subjects, yet both so pure, so simple...so childlike.

She didn't allow me to go home from that "first chat" empty handed. I became the recipient of one of her sweet potato pies, made earlier that day. I thought, as I walked down her driveway toward my humble abode, that there was probably nothing store-bought in this tasty dessert besides sugar. And had Horace planted a cane field, she'd have grown that, too.

My mind replayed her story concerning the origin of the name for Smackass Gap. I secretly thought they should have gone with the tale of the fat lady, for it would have been much more interesting and entertaining. And with a name like Smackass Gap, with its very own Smackass Branch, the place needed a little spice. People came there looking for a bit of humor. And those that didn't began searching for it the minute they entered Clay County and saw all the wonderful names of settlements and communities.

I decided that no matter what the authentic account for the name Smackass Gap, I was going to recommend that the town's historian put the one about the fat lady in his next book, *Clay County*

Tales.

That ought to be good for a few copies. I snickered, much like Miz Eudora had done when she mentioned the story about the fat lady. *In fact, I'd stand in line to get the first one!*

I laughed aloud, for I knew that would be the only way I'd find out about that story.

That's how it was that I came to feel "right at home" in Smackass Gap.

FIVE

Smarty Britches Make Hot Seats

BY THE MORNING after Horace's death, the word had apparently spread through the hollers and hills surrounding Smackass Gap, for neighbors began to trickle in. Not one of them came empty handed. Each bore a cake, a pie, a pot of chicken-n-dumplings, a large bowl of vegetables, cornbread, biscuits or some other succulent dish synonymous with the Appalachians. It quickly became obvious that everything that came through the door had been made from scratch, or grown in a garden right there in Clay County.

As I stood greeting each person at the front door, my contribution to Miz Eudora – since I knew better than to cook around all the kitchen experts of "these here parts" – I wondered who was going to eat this bountiful influx of food. After all, Horace was no longer around to help. It seemed a great waste as containers began to pile higher and higher on the kitchen counters and dining table.

I did notice, when I arrived at seven that morning, that Miz Eudora had not made her usual pan of biscuits. The enamel coffee pot sat on one of the two burners of the wood-burning stove in the kitchen and a bowl of scrambled eggs had just been "dished up" from the skillet on the other burner.

Now I was beginning to understand why she hadn't filled the kitchen and the back of the house with the usual aromas it held. She must have anticipated the neighborhood's reaction to her husband's death. Sure, I'd had a few things brought over following Leon's death, but those paled in comparison to the cornucopia of what was arriving here. I couldn't help but wonder whether a part of this was the women each trying to outdo the other. But as I took the containers, wrote down the name of each contributor on the booklet that had been left by Smiley Funeral Parlor, and found a place for them in the kitchen, I saw that this was a genuine outpouring of love for a neighbor in need.

One of the reasons for that deduction came as I reflected on the fact that Miz Eudora was known to be the best cook in all of Clay County. That meant she wasn't necessarily "in need," but the nearby residents were more in need of showing their respect for one of their own. It was a part of their upbringing, their breeding. A part of the reason I had come to so dearly love Smackass Gap.

The fact that so many of them looked alike gave me an opportunity to try to figure out more about the breeding of many of those who came to call. There was no pretense about anyone who showed up at the door that morning, quite unlike some of the people who showed up at Leon's wake. It became a game for me to try to figure out which fine, upstanding family – most of them founders of Clay County – each person belonged to.

I'd done fairly well at matching persons with their families until one rather large, *and rather unattractive*, woman knocked at the door. I noticed, as I opened the screen door slightly, that her silver Buick didn't resemble most of the other vehicles around Chunky Gal Mountain. There was no dust on her car, which appeared so new that I was sure had I opened the door, it would have still had that "new car" smell.

"I'm Mabel Jarvis…Mrs. John *G* Jarvis." Her voice dripped with a polite, Southern drawl. "I've come to console Eudora."

That announcement was my next signal that this woman wasn't a local. Otherwise she would have come to console "Miz" Eudora, especially given that they appeared to be near the same age.

"I'm her sister-in-law. I'm sure she's told you all about me."

That was my third, and most important, signal. I'd never once heard Miz Eudora mention *any* sister-in-law, much less Mabel Jarvis. I knew this was one guest the bereaved was not going to care to see. I stood there, peering at her two-piece tweed suit, it's rust color totally unbecoming to her charcoal gray hair, which I was sure came out of a bottle. Racing around her shoulders was a three-fox stole ensemble, with the little creatures' heads strung one after the other. She looked like a church lady straight out of the 1950s. Her jeweled broach and matching earrings, not to mention her designer-heeled shoes, were a clear indication that this woman was most assuredly *not* a frequent shopper of the area, and she certainly did not fit the stereotypical citizen of one of the unpretentious nearby communities.

Picturing her in the same room as Miz Eudora, *sister of Horace or not*, I sensed the next few minutes at the Rumph house might feature more sparks than the noted July 4th "dam fireworks" show at Lake Chatuge. I debated suggesting that she come back this evening when the family would be receiving friends at Smiley Funeral Parlor, but since she *was* departed Horace's family, I decided that wasn't a viable option. My mind raced in its attempt to find a way to prevent an unpleasant situation.

"Is Eudora here?" Mabel asked.

"Uh…yes…yes, she is," I stammered. "But she's with someone at the moment," I quickly added. "I believe she's working on plans for the funeral," I added with crossed fingers behind my back. *Maybe she's looking through "that blamed old cedar chest" for her black wool dress. That would be planning for the funeral,* I reasoned, trying to excuse my lie.

"Then I should be in there with her," the woman stated firmly. "Eudora doesn't have enough sense to plan a decent service or burial for Horace." Mabel started to plow past me, but I caught her elbow and turned her slightly, which was quite a chore, as I moved onto the porch with her.

"Did you see her beautiful array of fall mums as you drove up?" I asked, trying my best to shoo her away.

"I could care less about her mums or any other of her flowers. I have my gardener take care of those details for me so that all I have to do is enjoy their beauty in the cut flower arrangements he places in my home." The sweetness in her voice was gone.

I could care less... I'd already surmised that
from her appearance, much less her attitude. Those
words had been unnecessary, but they simply served
to prove my point.

"Look here, Mrs….," Mabel began, her face
flustered as she realized she didn't know my name,
"Mrs. 'Whoever You Are,' I came to see Eudora
and I'm going to see her." With that, she shoved
past me and stomped through the house, her designer
heels clapping against the floorboards and her head
bobbing, with an air of superiority, as she went in
search of her sister-in-law.

I followed, not sure whether in an effort to
help or whether I didn't want to miss the upcoming
tirade, of which I was sure both women would be
an active participant. I'm sure Miz Eudora heard
Mabel's approach, but she made no attempt to greet
her.

"My dear Eudora," Mabel began, her voice
again oozing with that same sappiness she'd first
tried on me.

"Land sakes, Mabel, what in heaven's name
are you doing here?" Eudora retorted.

Ah, the prequel to the sparks, I thought.

"I've come to help you with Horace's funeral
service," Mabel announced. She stood there, an all-
knowing expression in her eyes that matched the

tight smile on her lips.

"I don't need any help from you," replied Miz Eudora in no uncertain terms.

"Well, funerals are expensive, you know," reminded Mabel.

"I'm sure I can handle it," Miz Eudora stated. "Remember, here in the mountains, we take care of our own. We don't use them high-dollar machines to bury our dead."

"Surely you don't intend to dig the grave yourself?" Mabel asked indignantly.

"Well, I might!" exclaimed Miz Eudora. "Besides, the men folk here pitch in to help. They roll their shirtsleeves up after the service and start digging. There's usually at least six or seven sets of good hands, the same ones as what acts as pallbearers."

"You expect my brother to dig Horace's grave?" Mabel questioned, her outrage apparent.

"Absolutely not!" rebuked Eudora. "I don't even expect your brother to come."

She doesn't even want her brother-in-law, Horace's own brother, to come? I stared at the pair, quite puzzled by the fact that Miz Eudora had never once mentioned all these relatives, now materializing like some sort of bad spirit. Moreso, I had no idea what was going on here, but there was a world of difference between these two women. *And their attitudes,* I quickly noted. I could tell that Mabel Jarvis' visit was the beginning of an exciting next few days.

Not to worry, Sadie. She'll be gone the minute Horace is in the ground and she feels her social graces are no longer needed. I tried to hide the smirk I felt inside. *Too bad she can't sense that her social graces are no longer needed now.* I must admit, however, that I was a bit shocked that Miz Eudora didn't want Horace's family to be involved, no matter what had happened between them in the past. After all, they *were* blood kin.

"Now Eudora...,"

Oh no! The prequel is over, I realized. *We're getting ready for some serious fireworks.* I knew that any sentence that began with the word "Now" and was followed by someone's name was not going to be welcome. Especially to Miz Eudora Rumph. She wouldn't stand for anyone telling her what to do or how to do it, and particularly not this woman.

"...I know you're upset right now, with the sudden loss of Horace," continued Mabel. "You'll be thinking better before long. It's just too bad that your younger brother isn't still alive to talk some sense into you."

Watch out, Sadie, I warned myself as the

first bottle rocket went soaring. *This woman might have a fur, jewels and a Buick, but she surely doesn't know the way to win friendship and influence Miz Eudora.* There was no doubt that Mabel Jarvis was a prime example of an "in-law." *Or should I say "out-law,"* I smirked.

"John G. might have been my younger brother," Eudora stated, "and I did love him, but he couldn't tell which end was up, even if he *was* a proctologist. If he could have, he'd a'never married you. It's too bad that someone wasn't around to talk some sense into him before your wedding. Otherwise, you wouldn't be standing here in my way today."

There went the next explosion, I noted, wondering whether I should cover my head. Then the aftershock of her words struck me. Mabel Jarvis wasn't Horace's sister. She'd been married to Eudora's brother, so in all reality, there was no blood kinship to the deceased. I wondered whether I should save everyone the trouble of the next few days and usher her to the door, but I wasn't fast enough for those two.

"If I'd not married John G., he might have been stuck in Smackass Gap for the rest of his life," Mabel reasoned.

"And what would have been wrong with

that?" Miz Eudora asked. "He'd have done just fine
here as a doctor 'cause I heard a man once say that
everybody has two things: an opinion and an ..."

"Miz Eudora," I hastily interjected, "I believe
there's someone at the front door to see you." As I
took her arm to lead her away, I prayed that God
might send another neighbor, no matter that the
Rumph household didn't need any more food. He
did much better than that, for as we approached the
front room, I saw Preacher Jake coming up the steps
of the porch.

*Now that's what I call service, God! This
is even better than someone bearing food.* I
thought of the minister's impeccable timing, now
two days in a row. *Surely he can calm the brewing
storm between these two women,* I determined as
I again envisioned the image of "Touchdown Jesus."

"Good morning, Miz Eudora. You're looking
as lovely as one of your fall flowers."

*Maybe Mabel Jarvis should come in here
and hear the proper way to greet people,* I
pondered as I watched the tight lines on Miz
Eudora's face ease into a pleasant smile. Then I
remembered Mabel's statement from a few minutes
before. *"I don't care..."* This man cared about Miz
Eudora's flowers *and* her soul. *Not to mention
her heart and the rest of her,* I assessed, feeling

the generous warmth of his spirit all the way to my own soul.

Sensing this man had everything under control, I went back to my station of greeting visitors, taking food to the kitchen and keeping the register of who brought what. The pot of coffee emptied as I poured a mug – Miz Eudora didn't have cups, she used stoneware mugs that held a "healthy size serving" – for Preacher Jake.

As I took it to him, with cream and sugar the way he'd had it the evening before, I caught a glimpse of a figure approaching the porch steps. Seeing that it was Mabel, I went on to the living room and delivered the coffee, sure that she could let herself back in.

"Could I bring you some coffee, too, Miz Eudora?" I offered.

"Yes, thank you kindly," she answered, trying to regain her composure. "That blooming Mabel T. Jarvis is enough to drive anyone to drinking."

Preacher Jake and I each smothered a laugh as Miz Eudora continued. "If I knew where Horace kept his private stash, I'd pour a little 'shine in her coffee, and we'd be rid of her 'til this is all over."

"Helloooo," came a pleasant voice from the front door.

I went to greet the newest visitor, but saw

that it was Mabel. *Did she not let herself back in? Is she planning to make another grand entrance?* I wondered. *Maybe she didn't think one was enough.* If I'd known where Horace's private stash was stored, I'd have been tempted to put her out of *our* misery myself.

As I held the door open for her, I saw that she had removed her fur "chain of creatures." *So that's why she was outside. She took that ridiculous thing to the car.* I nearly laughed aloud at the thought of how many critters around Chunky Gal Mountain would have been glad to rid her of that garment. *Too bad one of those foxes didn't bite her on the way to the car. If we'd have been lucky, it would have been rabid and she'd be out of our way for sure.* Given the fact that God had just answered my prayer by sending Preacher Jake, I promptly withdrew that thought.

Mabel made her way toward the direction of chatter in the living room. As I followed her, I noticed that not only was the fox stole gone, but that she had also changed her entire wardrobe, including jewelry and shoes. This time, dressed in a simple, olive green dress and tan pumps, she could have actually passed for someone from the downtown church in Hayesville, the county seat of Clay County.

Trying to blend in, huh? Boy, she really **is** *ready for Round Two!* I decided. I was tempted to ask a few of the men visiting if they had an idea of where I might find Horace's stash.

"Eudora, dear, I was so saddened to hear the news," she sympathized the minute she saw Miz Eudora. She rushed over to the bereaved woman and placed her arms around her sister-in-law.

I was glad I'd not gotten myself a mug of coffee, for at this moment, it would have been splattered all over the walls. *What is with this woman?* my mind questioned. *Even her voice isn't as drippy as before. She almost sounds sincere.* I looked at Preacher Jake. This "man of the cloth" was obviously more of a miracle worker than I'd imagined.

The harsh lines around Mabel's mouth didn't seem quite as harsh as before and her piercing eyes had mellowed to a tranquil shade of hazel. Observing the transformation that had come over this woman, I felt like I was in one of those television scenes when the character wonders if she's walked into the wrong room. This was certainly not the atmosphere of the fireworks from a few minutes ago.

I felt like an introduction was in order for the minister, so I courteously interjected with, "Preacher

Jake, this is Eudora's…," I stopped, afraid I'd be forever shunned if I called the woman standing beside me her sister-in-law. My speech was further halted by the appearance of Mabel T. Jarvis from the bedroom.

Suddenly, for the second day in a row in this house, I felt a weakening in my knees, followed by a queasiness in my stomach. My head turned from side to side, glaring at the two women who could have been twins. *Identical twins at that,* I noted.

"Melba, what are you doing here? I didn't expect you to arrive so soon," said Mabel.

"I figured you'd be here, so I thought Eudora might need me. I knew someone would need to be here to keep you out of her hair."

Oops, the fireworks seem to be making a comeback! I feared.

"Sadie, Preacher Jake," Miz Eudora began, "this is Melba."

"Melba Toast," the woman said energetically, a huge smile plastered on her face and her head bobbing up and down. All she needed was a missing front tooth and she could have passed as some little kid at the front door yelling, "Trick or Treat.!" But we didn't have either a Trick or a Treat. We had a Toast. Melba Toast, a fact that appeared to make her "mighty proud."

"She's an old maid," Miz Eudora explained. "Never did get married. She's Mabel Jarvis' sister. Mabel was married to my baby brother, John G. Poor thing," she said, shaking her head. "Papa always said Brother lost it after he went away to college. Otherwise, he wouldn't a' got suckered in by her. Too bad Mabel wasn't a lot more like Melba. That's what Mama always said. Poor brother got the ugly one."

I wasn't sure how "Mama" could have told. They both looked the same to me.

A welcome knock at the door interrupted the painful introduction at exactly the very instant I saw Mabel opening her mouth for a comeback. I made my way to accept another dish of food on Miz Eudora's behalf when my eyes stopped, stuck on the man standing at the front door.

"Don't tell me," I mumbled slowly while looking bug-eyed, in what I know must have been a terribly stunned expression, at the man wearing a cream-colored turtleneck sweater and brown plaid polyester trousers. "You must be Mr. Toast."

"Yes," he replied, opening the door while I stood there, totally dumbfounded. "I am. Milton T."

Milton T? I found myself wanting to repeat. *Toast? Your name is Milton T. Toast?* It was a struggle keeping that question to myself, much less the chuckle that accompanied it. *And I thought Melba Toast was bad.* I winced. *And she even had a chance to get married and change her name.*

"Let me take you to where the rest of the family is gathered," I offered, feeling somewhat like a zombie-butler in a haunted mansion where all the guests look alike.

As I led Milton T. into the living room and looked at the three identical faces, I couldn't help thinking that it was Melba's name, and certainly not her looks, which was her claim to fame. My stare moved to Mabel. *The ugly one, huh?* I was sure at that youthful age of her marriage, and before Milton T. had grown bald, it would have been even more difficult for Mama to tell.

One glance at Preacher Jake showed that he shared my bewildered expression. For there stood three individuals, their faces each as round as a basketball, all with eyes that resembled small hazel-colored beads glued on their heads. The only feature that was strikingly different between any of them was that Milton T. did not have hair. Otherwise, they would have looked exactly alike.

Mabel didn't carry her weight nearly as well as Melba, nor her composure as well as Milton T. *But then, having to go through life, especially grade school, with a name like Milton T. Toast would have been bad enough to develop composure in any child*, I reasoned, still staring in disbelief at the trio. I think the majority of my shock came from having had no forewarning about them.

"So, Miz Eudora," Preacher Jake finally managed, "is this all of your family?"

"Land sakes, no!" she exclaimed. "Mabel might have been married to my baby brother, John G., and she, Melba and Milton T. are identical triplets, well, exceptin' for the plumbing, but they're not *my* family. That misfortune went to the grave with John G. It's buried somewhere down in Charlotte."

Miz Eudora leaned forward, but was unable to mask her voice enough to keep the rest of us from hearing her next words. "You know, it's too bad. They never were much to look at. I'll bet they weren't even cute when they were three little Toasts."

Preacher Jake lowered his head, trying to pretend a sneeze into his handkerchief.

Apparently all Melba heard was "three little Toasts" for she lightheartedly added, "When our mama was pregnant, the joke was that she had 'bread in the oven.'"

"Yep!" Milton T. nodded his head, picking

up on the tale. "She didn't know there was more than one of us until we 'popped out of the toaster!'" He and Melba each gave a hearty laugh. "Put, put, put," he mouthed, his pointer finger motioning in a different direction with each "put" and a loud percussive "p" on the front of each sound.

So much for the fireworks, I surmised. *This batch certainly was a dud.* I couldn't help but laugh at my own pun, *a batch of toast*, which was all right since there was now a roomful of laughter from all who had come from the kitchen to check on the commotion.

The look on Mabel's face, however, alerted me that this battle was not over yet.

"I think I heard someone else at the door," I lied as I quickly shuffled out of the room. Once I got around the corner, I stopped, holding my head close enough to hear the rest of the conversation and watch her actions.

"Preacher Jake," I heard Mabel say, her voice instantly cutting through the amusement of the room and halting all laughter. "I'm here to make sure that Eudora gives Horace a suitable burial. You know what I mean, I'm sure."

"Yes, I am sure," he replied. "I'm sure that *you* want to make sure that his memorial service and burial meet up to *your* social standards."

She nodded, noticeably grateful that this mountain preacher didn't need any further explanation. "I'm glad you see things my way," she continued.

Before she was able to finish her sentence, Preacher Jake interrupted. "I'm sorry, Mrs. Jarvis, but it isn't your way that matters here. Miz Eudora is the widow of Horace Rumph, and it is up to her to make sure that her husband's last wishes are upheld through this time of sorrow."

"Well, it will surely be a sad state of affairs if we leave *her* to handle this," Mabel replied, fuming on the rise in her voice. "She knows nothing about a celebration."

"Mabel, the minister is right," Milton T. spoke up. "Besides, you didn't ask, nor take, any advice about John G.'s memorial service."

"That's right, Mabel!" agreed Melba. "Otherwise *The Charlotte Observer* would not have run that dreadful obituary you wrote. It was so embarrassing that I could hardly stand to go and face the bridge club for months afterward. I still have friends laughing about that after all these years."

"How much did you have to pay to have that ridiculous mockery of a man's life run?" asked Milton T.

"None of your business," Mabel replied curtly, reaching into her purse and retrieving a business-sized envelope. "It wasn't *that* bad," she defended, her comment now aimed at Preacher Jake. "It really wasn't." She whipped a newspaper clipping from the envelope. "Here, see for yourself. I'm sure an educated man like yourself will see the value of it and agree that I should compose the one for Horace."

Preacher Jake politely took the clipping to appease Mabel, but only – I was sure – to keep the situation from these two women from becoming more volatile. I had no idea what the paper said, but from the expression of his eyes and mouth as his eyes scanned downward, I found myself wishing he'd read the document aloud.

John G. was Miz Eudora's baby brother. Maybe she'll have a copy I can read. I glanced at the shriveled-up expression on her face. From that, solely, I knew the chances of her having anything that Mabel T. Jarvis had "a hand in" was highly improbable.

Mabel, on the other hand, beamed from ear to ear as Preacher Jake read her "expository" on the life of John G. Jarvis.

Dr. John G. Jarvis, prominent and well-known

Charlotte proctologist, passed suddenly on the evening of April 1 at Presbyterian Hospital in Charlotte. Dr. Jarvis died of a blocked intestine caused by a kink in his upper colon, a dreadfully painful malady. It is believed the kink was caused by a slip of his proctoscope during a self-examination performed the day before. He recently had a succession of impactations.

Dr. Jarvis was born on Sept. 11, 1931 in Smackass Gap, NC to Merton Melvin Jarvis and Anna Eudora Peay Jarvis. He graduated valedictorian from the former Smackass School on Schoolhouse Hill, now Burnt Schoolhouse Road, where he developed a love for getting to the bottom of things leading him to study proctology. To pursue his dream of opening the largest proctology practice in the South, he earned his B.S. degree in Biology at University of North Carolina and his medical degree at Duke University where he was seated number one in his class. He was certified by the American Osteopathic Board of Proctology.

Dr. Jarvis was a pioneer in medicinal colon cleansing. His combination of 11 herbs and spices taken as a suppository anally brought life to colons all across the United States. When he added peppermint oil to his rectal paste he remarked, "It makes me feel like a York Peppermint Patty inside!"

Dr. Jarvis was known cheerfully by his patients as a gentle touching man with slender fingers. Many remarked after his examinations, "You never knew he was in there!"

Dr. Jarvis married the love of his life, Hickory (NC) socialite Mabel Toast on June 31, 1956. They had no children, though not from the lack of trying. Dr. Jarvis adored his lovely wife, Mabel, showering her with the finest things money could buy. Her social standing took on a higher level of prominence when he founded the John G. Jarvis Proctology Clinic in Charlotte. Dr. Jarvis was always proud of his wife who was the social bumblebee of the Myers Park Country Club of which he was an irreplaceable member.

Dr. Jarvis is survived by his darling wife, Mabel T. Jarvis, of the home; older (much older) sister, Eudora (Mrs. Horass) Rumph of Smackass Gap, NC; sister-in-law, Melba Toast of Charlotte and brother-in-law, Milton T. Toast of Hickory.

His body will lie in state on Friday from 9a.m. to 10p.m. in his favorite examination room at the John G. Jarvis Proctology Clinic where his family will receive a wide circle of friends and spectators. The funeral will be held at 11a.m. Saturday at St. Barnabass United Methodist Church in Charlotte.

The family kindly requests, in addition to the

generous sharing of flowers for the grave, that memorials be made to the Mabel T. Jarvis Trust Fund.

Preacher Jake examined the photo that accompanied the obituary and then glanced at the top of the clipping to see that it was dated April 3, 1984. He handed it back to Mabel with a pained expression on his face. I wasn't sure whether the source of that expression was a sympathetic reaction to the cause of Dr. John G.'s death, which Miz Eudora had mentioned earlier, or whether the article was that bad. Given the conversation that followed, I gathered it was the latter.

"I must admit, Mrs. Jarvis, that this is quite an article and it certainly held my interest." Preacher Jake cleared his throat. I could see the cautiousness written on his face, all the way from where I was standing, as he spoke his carefully selected words. "But as you must know, Horace Buchanan Rumph was a simple man, void of flowery words and showy actions. I believe his obituary should convey such a life. For John G., I'm sure this spoke to those who knew him."

"It spoke to people all right," Milton T. whispered to Melba. "They thought he was an idiot after they read that concoction, both those that knew him *and* those that didn't. It didn't help matters that Mabel was the worst speller of our litter. As much as she paid to have that cockamamie story printed, you'd have at least thought the newspaper would have edited it."

"And that bit about the friends and spectators," Melba replied, her voice not as quiet as Milton T.'s had been, "there were far more spectators than friends. The friends were too embarrassed to be seen there, but there were sure plenty of people who came by to gawk at our John G. after reading that obituary."

"Honestly, Mabel," Milton T. asked, "how could you hold your head up at that country club after that? I can't believe you weren't the laughing stock of Myers Park! Social bumblebee...humph! I'm surprised they didn't invite you to take a flight with that bumblebee."

Melba laughed so hard that she gave a little snort. " Yes, it would have been a faster flight than Rimsky-Korsakov's *Flight of the Bumblebee*."

The fact that Milton T. was bowed over in laughter, having joined in with Melba, gave Mabel exactly enough time to jump back into the conversation.

"But Preacher Jake," she said, trying to gain control of the situation.

"Peppermint patty, indeed," Milton T. scoffed, this time not in a whisper, but instead directed straight at Mabel. "Anonymous persons would occasionally leave peppermint patties on my desk until the day I retired after that article ran. Huh!" he huffed indignantly. "On the day I retired, someone placed an entire bag of those things beside my plate at my retirement luncheon. I'm surprised they didn't give me a gold-plated York Peppermint Patty for my going away gift!"

"Not to mention the eleven herbs and spices," chimed Melba, continuing the attack. It sounded like poor John G. worked for some fast food chicken chain rather than being a fine upstanding doctor. Personally, I'm glad he was dead at the time. Otherwise, he'd have died of humiliation. Honestly! Mabel, what *were* you thinking?"

"What's worse," Milton T. explained, "was that the mention of paste made it sound as if he'd invented something to glue the colon shut rather than cleanse it!"

It no longer mattered that Preacher Jake had not read the obituary aloud. After this ongoing riff, I'd heard all I needed to know about the obituary of John G. Jarvis.

"But Preacher Jake," Mabel tried again, this time with her voice booming over the den of noise created by all the chuckling from Milton T.'s comment.

Before she could finish her defense, the moment I'd been waiting for arrived. "Now Mabel T. Jarvis, you listen to me and you listen to me good." Miz Eudora had leaned up on the edge of her chair and it was obvious that she wasn't backing off until one of them came out of the ring victorious.

All right, I silently cheered, as the finale segment of the fireworks show shot off with a bang loud enough to capture the attention of everyone in the crowd.

As I moved back to the doorway of the living room, so as not to miss any of the guaranteed firework spectacle, I saw everyone else who had gathered in the house do the same. This showdown was unmistakably going to be more than anyone had bargained for. Even Preacher Jake settled back in his chair for a good ringside seat. I debated whether I should bring out some of the food from the kitchen and sell concessions.

Mabel noticed, too, for she stuffed the obituary clipping back into her purse for safekeeping.

"You're not a'going to put in the paper what Horace died of," ordered Miz Eudora. "Besides, it surely wasn't from a blocked intestine like John G.

We all knowed he was full of it, but you didn't have to go and blab it to the world."

"And just how do you know that Horace didn't have a blocked intestine?" Mabel asked.

"Because he took the new slop jar out right a'fore he went to pick the apples," Miz Eudora admitted, giving a bit more detail than most people in the room wanted to hear. "You know what they say: 'An apple a day keeps the doctor away,' and it sure don't hurt your intestines either."

"Well, maybe he had tick fever or something," Mabel said, digging for possibilities.

"P'SHAA!" exclaimed Miz Eudora. "He was so ornery that the tick would have died. Besides, I 'spect Horace had taken a little nip the night before, so the tick would have passed out before it got a chance to bite him.

"And not only that," she ranted on, "you're not a'going to tell everything that Horace done his whole life. Who wants the world to know everything they done? Why, that's like putting it all up on a movie screen for everybody to see. There might be a few things that Horace done that he didn't get caught for, so there's no need to dredge them up now."

"Amen, sister!" came a spirited cry from the back of the room.

One of Horace's drinking buddies, I figured. *Maybe he'd know where the stash is and we can end this before it becomes a knock-down, drag-out.* But one look at Miz Eudora convinced me that was a bad idea. She was venting a lot of grief through this outburst and I had no intention of getting in the way of such a good therapy session. Being married to a counselor all those years had taught me a few things. I suspected that years of biting her tongue, for John G.'s sake, were taking this opportunity to unleash, too, though I had a hard time imagining this strong mountain woman biting her tongue for anything or anybody.

What I did know for a fact was that the spirited man's acclamation was good enough to give Eudora Rumph a second wind, for I saw her rear back to take another verbal blow at her "sister-in-law."

"Every newspaper in the land would be wanting to find out the special ingredients of Horace's special recipe by the time you got through. Then I'd have them G-Men crawling the place again and tearing up all the barns and haystacks looking for stills."

I heard a couple of panicked gasps echo off the walls, which could have been misconstrued as "oohs" and "aahs" over the fireworks, but I knew immediately that Miz Eudora's comment had struck a chord with a few of Horace's buddies.

"As far as I'm concerned, Horace's sideline business will be buried with him, just like that misfortune of John G. bringing these identical triplets into our family was buried with him."

I couldn't help but notice that Miz Eudora was picking up steam and was ready to lay in for another round.

Melba saw it, too, for she took Mabel's arm. "Why don't Milton T. and I take you home? I'm sure this is a painful time for you as it must remind you of your own loss of John G.."

"That's a great idea," said Milton T. "We can stop at that little biscuit café on the way and give the owner a hard time about how toast is better than biscuits, just like we used to."

I saw a glimmer of excitement on Melba's face. "That would be fun, wouldn't it, Sis? Although I must admit that I've never had a bad biscuit in that place."

"Sounds like the Hayesville Family Restaurant," came a comment from another corner of the room. "I don't think its owner, Tommy Hooper, knows what a bad biscuit is."

"Biscuits and gravy, umm-umm," added a gent, licking his chops. "That's my favorite thing on the menu."

"I saw a mess of biscuits in the kitchen," said one of Horace's friends. "I'm sure if we look hard enough, we can find some gravy in one of them bowls on the table."

I knew "a mess" meant a bunch, and the man was right, for practically every cook in Smackass Gap had sent over biscuits with a bowl of something to go with them.

Everyone's face – except for Mabel's, that is – lit up when Miz Eudora offered, "And if there's not any gravy, why, I can whip some up some chocolate gravy in no time."

I'd heard a few of the women around Hayesville speak of chocolate gravy, but I'd not yet had the good fortune of tasting it. It was made especially to go with biscuits, but it was only served on special occasions, "like Sundays and such." *And celebrations of life,* I noted, excited that I might finally get my first taste of chocolate gravy.

"You know," Miz Eudora continued, "I remember when Tommy's mama, Cleo, taught him how to make gravy when he was just a little young'un. He'd walk over here with her and we'd all string beans together on the back porch. Now there's a boy what knows that you work on the back porch and relax on the front porch. He always was a good little worker. If I'd had a son, I'd have liked for him to be just like Tommy."

While Miz Eudora led the procession to the kitchen and the banquet of food, Mabel made a beeline toward the front door, with Melba and Milton T. following closely behind her, proverbial gravy on the faces of the Toasts. As I watched the trail of dust from their cars, I realized that, for the first time in my life, I was glad for toast – which I'd never cared for unless it was Jewish rye, and it was obvious that none of the Toast family was of that origin.

This time of celebration had truly gotten off to a lively start, and had been anything but somber and sad for Eudora Rumph.

I caught Preacher Jake on the way to the kitchen. "You know, those three may become the Toasts of the town before it's all said and done."

"That's a good one," he said with a grin. "I think I may use that in Horace's obituary. 'Mabel T. Jarvis, Melba and Milton T. – named the Toasts of Smackass Gap following their visit to the home of the deceased.' I really don't think Miz Eudora would mind. It would be like giving her, or rather Horace, the last word."

I liked this man more all the time. God had been gracious in having him for Miz Eudora's preacher in this time of need, a fact for which I thanked Him during the blessing Preacher Jake offered over the biscuits and other food in the kitchen. I also gave Him thanks for biscuits, and for bread in the oven, or toaster, or wherever. *"Put, put, put,"* I mimicked silently, flicking my pointer finger in different directions, at the end of the prayer.

It seemed everyone in Smackass Gap helped themselves to a round of biscuits and gravy, topped off by a round of Miz Eudora's chocolate gravy. The Toasts had been quite an appetizer, for they stirred up a lot of hunger, I mused as I washed all the dishes from the banquet in Horace's honor. *Or memory*.

*Maybe there **is** some merit to that tale of this place being named after a fat lady rather than the old mining wagons being pulled by mules*, I noted with an audible chuckle as I thought about the "fat lady" going up against the "mule-headed" sister-in-law.

That's how it was that I came to learn that smarty "britches," as they call pants in Smackass Gap, make hot seats. For Mabel's was surely on fire as she "hightailed" it out of Clay County that afternoon. I could hardly wait for the morrow.

"Smarty britches make hot seats, smarty britches make hot seats," I sang over and over in a sing-song fashion as I walked home to choose something, a bit more colorful than originally intended, to wear for the next day's celebration of the life of Horace Buchanan Rumph.

SIX

A Smile to Remember

AT FIRST, I had scolded myself for volunteering to be Miz Eudora's chauffeur for the funeral, but after yesterday's episode with Mabel, I decided my suggestion had been a monumental stroke of genius. Miz Eudora had not wanted to ride in the family car, citing that she had "no intention of being caged up in the same vehicle as Mabel, Melba and Milton T." and that "riding in that big ole black automobile was only one step away from riding in the hearse yourself."

She does have a point! I'd reasoned to myself, visualizing a funeral procession with the hearse and the family car, one behind the other.

"Besides," she'd concluded, "why in tarnation do I want to spend that much money when I can just as easily walk down to Smiley Funeral

Parlor and then back up the mountain to the church? Why, I've walked to church many a Sunday," she reminded me. "If Horace was a little too done from the night before, I'd go to church by myself. It was just a little hike compared to walking this whole farm."

Given the fact that between Horace's family and her family, they owned at least six hundred acres, I figured "as to how" she had a point. Still, I insisted that she allow me to drive her on the day of the big celebration. At the time, I'd found it remarkably touching that even in her grief, Miz Eudora had brought a light moment to my life. I was glad to be able to give some small gift of myself to her in return.

Now, though, as I drove up her long driveway to take her for one final viewing at Smiley's, and then the service at the church, I again dreaded my decision. Each foot seemed like a mile. I wasn't sure what it was that made it seem such, but I suspected it was my sorrow for her situation. I knew the pain she would have to bear once this day of celebration was over. When she returned home following the service, that's when the loneliness and the heartache would set in. I knew... I knew, for mine was still there.

When I reached her house, she was waiting

patiently on the front porch. I had to rub my eyes to make sure that the person standing there was truly Miz Eudora and not some stranger who'd wandered through town. She had short curly hair, done up in a "new do" so frizzy that I wondered whether she'd gotten her finger stuck in a light socket. From her head to her toes, a transformation – if that's what you could call it – had occurred in the simplistic, "au natural" woman that I'd "spent many an afternoon with."

Her head was adorned with a large-brimmed red satin hat, with a bright purple satin flower and a piece of purple boa sticking on it for decoration. On her feet were red, orthopedic-looking shoes that reminded me of the "Old Mother Comforts" that my grandmother used to wear. She carried a red purse that matched the red leather of her shoes.

As I got closer, I saw that her glasses had a red and purple floral design on them, and she had on gaudy, purple dangling earrings. I knew she didn't have pierced ears, so I was surprised that the clips on those heavy things weren't pulling her ear lobes all the way down to her chin. Not to mention that it was probably the first time in Eudora Rumph's life that she'd worn "ear-bobs," especially dangly rhinestone ones! About the glasses, I had no idea what she'd used to fashion them, but I hoped she liked them, for I expected they were that way now for life.

Her dress was a hideous dark purple with blotches of red all over it, and to make matters worse, it had a big bow at the neck, which on her was all twisted and crooked. That was all right, though, for it matched the twisted and crooked appearance of her "stockings" which were held up on her legs with old-timey garters. As old as they were, I was stunned that they could hold up anything.

All of that was startling enough, but the real shocker was the purple fur coat she was wearing, with its collar of crocheted, sparkly purple yarn and a matching trim all the way down the front. To make matters worse, she had on two pins, one on each bosom, that had lights flashing on and off. They reminded me of a traffic warning sign.

Maybe that's what they are, I thought. *Warnings signs to let people know to get out of her way!*

I didn't know whether to open the passenger door for her, or to drive home as fast as I could and call Sheriff Bonner. *Or perhaps Preacher Jake. He could perform an exorcism!* I thought in horror.

But at that moment, my own transformation took place for I began to peered admirably at the vision before me. A few seconds earlier, I had decided that this "person" standing on the Rumph front porch truly *was* a transformation – from a plain, simple mountain woman to an elderly streetwalker! Now I saw her through "Miz Eudora eyes" (*minus the red and purple floral designed glasses!*) with the same spirit of a child that she possessed. In that light, she was a vision of loveliness, dressed in the most festive attire she could find – and heaven only knew where that was, for I'm sure these things weren't stored away in that "blamed old cedar chest!" – to celebrate the life of the man with whom she'd spent her adult life. *At least up until this point*, I reasoned.

Another glance at her told me that the transformation I'd been privy to preview was going to be the new Miz Eudora. Same soul, same heart, same irony, but different clothes. *"And remember, Sadie,"* I could hear Leon saying, *"clothes don't make the person. It's what's inside them that counts."* Even I had not yet encountered all the goodness that was housed inside this woman. *Nor the spunk!* I suspected.

I came to a stop and opened the car door, trying my best to find my voice. "Why, Miz Eudora!" I exclaimed. "I almost didn't recognize you in those clothes. Your fur coat is about the most…the most…stunning wrap I've ever seen."

"Isn't it a beauty?" she asked, running her fingers down the fur, smoothing out the nap as she did. "Lynnette, one of the sweet young mothers in the church brought me this piece of purple fur last evening and said she thought it might help keep me warm on the nights ahead. She called it a 'plush wrap.' I reckon she didn't figure that I'd be as warm as I ever was. Horace had his own special 'recipe' to keep him warm, you see." Miz Eudora had leaned toward me with that last statement as if it were some great secret.

"I never saw purple fur like this before. When that sweet young Lynnette handed it to me, I had to ask her what kind of fur it was. She called it 'faux fur' (pronounced fo-pher). I guess that's some kin to a gopher. Anyhows, whatever kind of animal it is, it sure does have a pretty coat of fur. I was so excited that I set right out to cutting it out to make myself a fur coat. That Mabel's not the only one in the family that can look fine and elegant for the funeral. I'll let her know I'm as good as her any old day." With that, Miz Eudora sat down in the passenger seat, making sure not to get her new 'wrap' caught in the door.

"It is most colorful," I finally managed. "It is sure to bowl Mabel Jarvis right over!"

"Good," she said, giving a simple giggle. "Maybe she'll be standing at the front door of Smiley's and we'll be rid of her to start with."

I hoped it didn't also bowl Milton T, over, for if it did, someone would surely mistake his bald head for a bowling ball and "head off" – not to make a pun – to the Hayesville Alley with him in short order.

"It was mighty neighborly of you to offer to drive me today," she said, "but I was still half a minded to walk to Smiley's this morning so that everybody could see my new coat. This celebration thing is turning out to be right much fun."

The laughter that had been, up until that point, carefully held inside now splattered all over the windshield. Any fears I'd had earlier about this being a dreadful day dissipated with the last few traces of morning dew. I sat back comfortably in the driver's seat, relaxed my hands on the steering wheel and took a long peaceful breath, sure that I would *not* return home all teary-eyed and reliving the grief brought about by my Leon's passing. Perhaps I would even have the freedom to celebrate his life during the course of this day.

The conversation on the rest of the way to Smiley Funeral Parlor was as light and carefree as it might have been had I been taking Miz Eudora to the grocery store, had she been someone who frequented the grocery store. We went to the funeral parlor briefly before going to the church so that she could see Horace one last time, as the casket would be closed at the church by the time she would lead the procession down the aisle to begin the service.

And what a grand procession it's going to be, I mused, envisioning her strutting in front of Mabel in her new purple "fo-pher" coat with those flashy things going off to light the way.

That's how it was that I came to learn that one has to not only love, but also laugh at one's self and the world around him or herself.

IT HAD BEEN my original intention to drop Miz Eudora off at the front entrance of Smiley Funeral Parlor and then park the car before joining her. But given the outrageousness of her "colorful" attire and new "look," I opted instead to find a spot near the door and walk in with her. I don't know why, for I should have come to realize that the last person in the world to need a bodyguard was Miz Eudora Rumph. Perhaps my reasoning came from a subconscious curiosity of not wanting to miss any of the excitement when she made her grand entrance. I even considered slipping her in through the back entrance, but after all the trouble she'd gone to in search of her "celebration" clothes, I decided she needed to make the biggest splash possible.

And what a big splash it was, for when Mabel Jarvis, who was standing at the water fountain, saw Miz Eudora come in the front door, her finger dropped all the way down on the push button, causing a huge spray of water to come up and hit her right in the face. The tall, slender undertaker who had visited the home grabbed a handful of tissues from the nearest box and handed them to her.

"Good heavens, Eudora!" Mabel exclaimed, wiping her face and her shoulders. "Where on earth did you find that ridiculous outfit?" Her eyes moved up and down her sister-in-law slowly, taking in every inch of the spectacle in front of her and stopping when her eyes reached Eudora's hair. "And what in the name of Sam Hill happened to your hair?"

"Isn't it great? I found an old Toni home permanent under the kitchen sink," explained Eudora.

"You what!" Mabel began to fan so hard with the paper fan provided by Smiley Funeral Parlor that I started to suggest she try another splash of water. "A Toni perm? Don't you know those things went out of style decades ago? Why, I haven't seen one of them in at least forty years!"

"No wonder it only had 89 cents marked on it. I bought it a long time ago…back in 1959…at the little country store Pa used to own…and I was saving it for a rainy day. But that little lady on the box was so pretty that I thought she looked more like a celebration than a rainy day."

"Don't tell me you did this all by yourself?" Mabel inquired.

"Sure did. It was a breeze compared to making icebox pickles, especially when you don't have much of an icebox."

Mabel's mouth hung open. "I can't believe it didn't burn every hair on your head off."

I snickered, suspecting that to be the reason Miz Eudora had a new horizontal stripe of light gray running sideways across the front of her hairline. She must have rinsed all the solution out just in time. Otherwise, I suspected she would have burned off all her hair. Frankly, I was impressed that there had been any curl at all left in the box. I didn't bother to inform either of them that the very first permanent was invented in 1906 and was a mixture of cow urine and water, a tidbit of useless knowledge I'd learned during the one class when I thought it might be fun to be a cosmetologist.

"And I found my dress down at a store called Goodwill. They had the fanciest things hanging up in the window. Reminded me of something you'd wear, though, Mabel, so I started not to go in."

I watched as Mabel's mouth fell open.

"But when I saw the name on the store was Goodwill," said Miz Eudora, "it reminded me of Mary and Joseph and the baby Jesus, and peace on earth. When I tried this on, I felt just like I was one of the characters in the Christmas pageant." Her smile was so big that I could almost imagine her as a child in the church's yearly drama.

"You're a character in costume, all right," replied Mabel, "but it isn't from any Christmas pageant. More like a horror movie, if you ask me."

"Well, I didn't ask you," Miz Eudora blurted, verbally putting her sister-in-law in her place. She then held out her red leather purse. "I could hardly believe my luck when I found this hanging on a stand on my way to pay for the dress." That's when she kicked out her right foot, catching Mabel's shin and this time physically putting her sister-in-law in her place. "Look here at how nice my shoes match it. I found them down at the Christian Love Ministries Store."

Before she had a chance to tell us the history, or the origin, of the hat, the funeral home director

approached us. "May I take your picture, Miz
Eudora, so that you might have something to
remember this day?" he asked courteously, his
toothy grin making him, too, a perfect candidate for
his position at Smiley Funeral Parlor.

Remember the day? I repeated to myself.
*How soon does he think she'll forget the death
of her husband?* I stared at the man in disbelief. *I
guess they don't teach morticians the fine art of
not sticking your foot in your mouth!* However,
as I looked at all the teeth in his mouth showing
through his smile, I realized there was little room
for anything else in his mouth. *Oh well, at least
he's a great poster child for the Smiley Funeral
Parlor. Perhaps they should keep him for the
advertisements and use someone else to console
the bereaved.* My ponderings were interrupted by
Mabel's ranting about the photograph.

"In that get up?" snapped Mabel. "Surely
you're kidding!"

"Oh, hush up," warned Eudora. "You're just
jealous 'cause you can't be in the picture."

No more than I had been around Mabel Jarvis,
I'd already figured out how much she relished being
in the limelight. Therefore, I reasoned that Miz
Eudora's statement was correct.

As the funeral home director methodically

positioned her beside the pump organ, that I suspected had been the very first musical instrument in the church of Smackass Gap, she politely asked, "Ain't it customary to take the picture of the widow beside the casket of the deceased?"

"Oh, no, Miz Eudora. That's considered morbid. This pump organ is a most beautiful backdrop for your exquisitely unique outfit."

She looked down and patted her fur coat. "Ain't it 'bout the best party garb you ever did see?"

"It's certainly the most outrageous attire I've ever seen," the director answered in such a respectful way that I had to cover my mouth with my embroidered linen handkerchief.

"Yep, the preacher said it was a celebration. I'm sure glad ever'body felt the way they did, seeing as how I was a-dreading getting that old black wool dress outta the cedar chest. That thing's been in thar so long, I bet it was good and ripe."

I wasn't sure whether the man was making light of Miz Eudora, or whether it really was the custom of the area to take the picture of the spouse of the deceased. Either way, that proud woman stood tall, clasped her new "used" red leather purse in her hand and gave him a smile, or should I say, "grin," that said, "I am who I am, I don't care whether you like it or not, and you'd better not mess with me."

She might not have said it exactly as wordy or as ladylike, but she'd have gotten the same point across, with that same smile that was now captured for eternity.

That's how it was that, for the second time, Miz Eudora taught me that there is life after death, and that it was time for me to give up my pity party and get on with mine.

SEVEN

A Final Farewell

ON A SCALE of one to ten, with ten being the highest, Horace's celebration of life scored a twelve from the moment Miz Eudora started down the aisle of First Church, Smackass. Heads that would have normally bowed in reverence darted back and forth from the image of her in that frock to those seated around them, all checking their neighbors' faces to see if they saw the same measure of disbelief. The usual sniffling of a memorial service had been traded for snickers of a festive occasion.

Given Miz Eudora's conception of "festive occasion" in the wardrobe department, I was surprised that the pews weren't adorned with balloons, nor that party horns hadn't been handed out by the ushers as mourners entered the church.

The occasion did became a bit more festive when I noticed that the garters, which I had wondered about from the beginning, gave way and her "stockings" fell down around her ankles about halfway down the aisle. I was impressed that she nonchalantly finished her grand entrance as if nothing had happened. I was more impressed that Mabel's mouth didn't hit the floor as she stared at the sight in front of her, but she didn't dare lose face in front of this crowd of people whom she was determined to impress.

However, as I took a closer look at Mabel, sacheting down the aisle directly behind Miz Eudora, I noticed that she indeed was making an impression for she'd lost more than her face. I'd been so interested in the reactions to Miz Eudora's attire at the Smiley Funeral Parlor that I'd failed to notice what Mabel had on. ***Or rather didn't have on!*** I now noted. It appeared that she'd gotten dressed in such a hurry to keep tabs on everything that she'd neglected to put on the skirt that went with her black suit. The black satin slip that she was wearing, however, was certainly pretty with its lace trim edging the bottom.

I wasn't a Biblical scholar, but I seemed to recall some verse about not worrying about the splinter in your neighbor's eye until you removed the log from your own. It seemed that could just as easily have been reworded to say, "Thou shalt not condemn your neighbor's clothing until you take a good look at your own."

I dared not look at Melba and Milton T. too closely for fear of what else I might see. *Or not see,* I corrected.

I'm sure there were a lot of bruises throughout the congregation by the time the family reached the front pews. That is, if all the elbows I saw go flying were any indication. It looked as if Miz Eudora got their attention and Mabel went in for the kill. *Even though that's not the best scenario to use at a funeral,* I admonished myself.

Preacher Jake looked down from the pulpit and winked at the bereaving widow, an act I deemed most appropriate in this case. I'm sure he'd never seen such an array of celebration, nor such a variety of mishaps, in all his years of ministry in Smackass Gap. *Or anywhere else for that matter!* I noted.

He then glanced out across the congregation as he shepherded them back into a tone of composure – *no small act and one for which he deserved a gold medal in this case!* – before leading them in a congregational reading of "The Shepherd's Psalm."

From that moment, he became one of my

"forever heroes," for there appeared a genuine appreciation in his eyes for both the uniqueness and the simplicity of the woman who sat before him. I'd not known many ministers in my lifetime, but Preacher Jake had instantly jumped to the top of the totem pole of holiness in my book. From what I'd observed on television and read in the newspapers of some of the scandalous "defrockments" lately, he was a jewel among men.

I forced my attention to stay honed in to the words of his eulogy for Horace, hoping for a bit of respite from my own loss. "And today," I heard him say, "we can all follow the wonderful example of Eudora Jarvis Rumph as she shows us what it means to fully celebrate the life of a loved one who has gone on to their ultimate reward."

Well, isn't that fine? Not only does he accept her appearance, he condones it in front of the "unbelievers" and "Pharisees," I thought bemused, as his eyes met those of Mabel. Preacher Jake was gaining points by the basketful.

I, myself, had watched her in a new light as she walked alone, her head held high, in front of the rest of the family of mourners, all of whom had created their own spectacle the day before at the Rumph home. *And one doing a good job today,* I immediately thought about Mabel. What struck me was that Miz Eudora's purple "fopher" coat captured the periwinkle blue of her eyes, a product of age from her once vibrant deep-blue eyes, in a way that made her entire face radiate in a warm, yet brilliant, glow. I wasn't sure if it was the hair, the eyes, the red lipstick or the fact that she was wearing bright, bold colors, but she exuded life.

Even after the processional music had ended, I couldn't take my eyes away from her. I decided that it was the combination of all the factors of her "get-up." And as awkward as it was to admit, given the outrageousness of her outfit, it was actually quite becoming on her. I was personally glad Preacher Jake had convinced her that this day was a celebration. As I watched her, and the effect the clothes had on her mood, I decided that it was my duty as her friend and neighbor to make sure that her old wardrobe be replaced with all bright colors. From that moment, it became my self-proclaimed responsibility to make sure that everyday was going to be a celebration for her.

The more I listened to the words of the minister, watched as Mabel scorned her sister-in-law, and observed Miz Eudora's handling of the day, it become apparent that she deserved this new lease on life. Rather than pray for her loss, I found myself thanking God that now it was her turn to delight in all He had given her. *A turn that is long overdue!*

As the choir stood and sang *In the Sweet By and By*, I imagined Horace waiting beside "that beautiful shore" in the words of the chorus. Waiting to meet his box lunch reward with her as colorfully enchanting and radiant as she was at this moment. While the choir continued with, "we will sing on that beautiful shore the melodious songs of the blest," I pictured him singing songs like he'd never sung at the rapturous vision of her.

Just about the time I started to get teary-eyed at the beauty of the moment, I noticed that Miz Eudora had bent over, not to blow her nose or wipe away tears, but to take off her orthopedic-looking red shoes and pull off those droopy stockings. When she straightened back up, I detected that one of the flashy pins on her coat had fallen off.

Oh, no, I said, in the form of opening words to a prayer as if God hadn't already noticed, while I feared the "sweet by and by" was about to have a new, and not so pretty nor melodious, ending. *Don't let that thing stick her. She's liable to let out such a blood-curdling scream that they'd have to peel us all off the ceiling.*

Sure that it had dropped down her bodice, I sat waiting patiently for her to discover it missing and fish it out, trying my best not to stare.

I also noticed Mabel squirming around like a cat on a hot tin roof. She was doing her best to gain a little attention, since Preacher Jake didn't kowtow to her desire to take over the arrangements. She got her big moment, for all of a sudden, she yelped and jumped up like a cat whose tail had been caught in a meat grinder instead of one on a hot tin roof. When she looked down and noticed her slip, she gave another rip-roaring yelp that outdid the first one.

The pin didn't go down Miz Eudora's dress, I decided, laughing like the rest of the congregation.

"What are you doing with my pin?" Miz Eudora asked accusingly, totally ignoring the absence of a skirt, when she saw it flashing from Mabel's backside.

That's when I realized that Miz Eudora had been so attuned to Preacher Jake's words, and the choir's music, that she hadn't even missed it. She hastily rescued the pin, reattached it to her lapel and went back to listening with all her might to the rest of the eulogy, periodically checking the whereabouts of her pins.

I was a bit disappointed that she had reached down and removed the stockings, garters and all, for I think it would have made quite a spectacle to watch her walk back out of the church and up the hill to the cemetery with them dragging the ground behind her.

Much to my surprise, the burial was short and sweet, I noted as I stood near the Smiley Funeral Parlor tent. I'd positioned myself at an angle where I could keep an eye on Miz Eudora and the three Toasts, not wanting to miss an iota of the action should they break into another entertaining squabble. But to everyone's chagrin, the hose were gone, the pins stayed in place and Mabel, whose black slip blended in with the black fold-up chairs, sat completely still.

I'd seen services where the pallbearers would each march by the casket and lay their lapel boutonnières on it as a last act of respect for the deceased. They had done that at Leon's service and I'd found it most touching. The touching moment of Horace's burial came, though, when after Preacher Jake's final "Amen" and he'd made his way down the two rows of survivors, Miz Eudora carefully removed her purple fopher coat, handed it to me and grabbed a shovel, covering the casket that was then lowered into the ground.

Where are my tissues when I need them? I screamed internally. I stood motionless as the men around her each grabbed a shovel from the beds of their pick-ups and began to help with the interment.

During this solemn procedure of bidding Horace a final farewell, I didn't bother to turn to see what the three Toasts were doing, for at that moment, they were nothing more than stale bread to me. The act before me was the most beautiful sight and the most touching tribute I had ever witnessed.

That's how it was that I came to learn that time really does march on, and I was sure that as soon as Miz Eudora piled on the last shovel of dirt and reclaimed her purple fopher coat, she would give Mabel Toast Jarvis her marching orders.

EIGHT

If Only I Had a Red Hat

I REMEMBERED ONCE hearing my sister, who'd been blessed with five children, laugh about how it must be a written rule that it rains at least once a day at amusement parks – usually at four in the afternoon just as the parade is getting ready to begin. Suddenly the entire park would converge into a sea of yellow as people donned their yellow slickers, and the ones who didn't have them rushed to the nearest gift shop to buy their own. The mass of yellow made it impossible to spot your own child. That's how it was the day I came to meet the Red Hatters in my quest for Miz Eudora.

We left the cemetery following Horace's burial and at Mabel's insistence-which should have immediately thrown up a red flag-instead of taking Miz Eudora immediately home, we decided to "go to town," no skirt and all, so that the lack of Horace's presence wouldn't haunt her in her "new state of widowhood."

Personally, I didn't think that new state of widowhood was going to be an issue for Miz Eudora, but since I'd made myself available as the chauffeur and not the event planner, I said nothing. Instead, I took her to Chinquapin's, a store that had become a tradition on the square of Hayesville, at her request for "a cone of butter pecan ice cream since this was a day of celebration."

"Would you look at that?" Miz Eudora asked as we entered the front door of what used to be Tiger's Cash Store and still served as a great dry goods store. She pointed to some rather odd-looking pottery faces on the shelves to the left of the store. "If those things had hair, they'd look just like Mabel." She snickered. "As it is, they look like Milton T."

I turned to see that she was right.

"That thing doesn't look like Milton T.," observed Mabel. "His nose isn't shaped like that."

I took off toward the other side of the store for a brief moment to hide my laughter. *Only one more day, Miz Eudora,* I wanted to say. *Only one more day and they'll be gone.*

We'd no more than gotten our scoops of ice

cream when Mabel began telling Miz Eudora how she needed to go about "the rest of the days of her life."

"Why, you…you…," Miz Eudora mumbled. "You don't even have the decency to wear a skirt to my husband's funeral and you want to tell me what to do? P'SHHA!"

Seeing a vision of the butter pecan cone plastered over Mabel's nose, I grabbed her arm and pushed her toward my car. "Mabel has decided to finish her sherbet at home," I declared as we left the bereaved sitting on the bench of the front sidewalk. Proud of myself for taking control of a dangerous situation and playing mediator, I called back, "I'll be back for you shortly."

Good one, Sadie! I congratulated myself. *Even Leon was never that forceful in his mediation work.*

"Don't bother," Miz Eudora yelled behind me. "I think I'd like to walk home alone."

As much as I hated leaving her on that bench, I knew that for the moment, anywhere she could be, without Mabel, was exactly where she needed to be.

"You know," Mabel began as we started back toward the motel, "that woman will never be able to get by on her own. I'm thinking of moving here to assist her."

The car stopped right in the middle of Highway 64 as I literally stood on the brake. "You're doing what?" I asked, unaware of the horns of impatient drivers blowing behind me.

I saw her mouth moving, but I heard no words as I sputtered, "Eudora Rumph is the strongest person I know. Had it not been for her, I'm not sure how I would have dealt with my own grieving during the past year. She's taught me to laugh and to live again."

My words stopped as the motive for this woman's move became clear. This place was growing tremendously in value, it was close to all the up-and-coming areas of Georgia, and since she still had acreage from John G.'s death, she could come to an area where she would be a big fish in a small pond.

That is, I thought, *unless we can find a way for her to fall into Lake Chatuge. She'd be such a small fish in that body of water that she'd never be found.* I caught myself in mid thought, realizing that I'd learned more from Miz Eudora than I'd suspected. *Including how to knock off Mabel!* I cringed.

"Furthermore," I stated emphatically, as the image of "that woman" ran through my mind, seated on that bench alone in that colorful attire licking away at her ice cream cone, "I'm sure if she set her mind to it, she could land the lead role in a production by the Licklog Players at the Peacock Theater!" I pressed the gas pedal. "And without your help!" I added as a coda.

Little did I realize that within five minutes after our departure, a busload of Red Hatters would converge on the town square of Hayesville and my "strong lady" would be swallowed up in a sea of red. Nor did I realize that within the next twenty-four hours, Miz Eudora would create her own lead role of her own production by the Red Hat Players aboard the Peacock Bus Lines.

"HURRY UP AND finish that last lick," warned a woman in a red hat, who took Miz Eudora by the arm. "You'll miss the bus if you don't come on. You know the routine. They won't wait on anyone, no matter whether you're the queen or the jester."

Before Miz Eudora had time to respond, another woman, also donning a red hat, grabbed her other arm. "C'mon, sweetie, I'll help you up the bus steps. We rocked a little too long on that front porch of The Dillard House when we stopped for lunch, so we didn't have nearly enough time for this stop." She saw the remnants of the cone. "Ooh, you're lucky. I didn't have time for an ice cream for looking in all the other shops."

Seeing the large group of women headed toward the bus, Miz Eudora quickly spotted an empty seat and took it while finishing the last bite of her cone. She settled back to enjoy the scenic ride home, thinking how much more spacious this was than the family car for which she could have opted.

"It sure does seem cramped in this bus," Marlene, the most svelte of the bunch on the bus, observed as she squirmed in her seat. She removed her stylish, floppy red hat, laying it in her lap, as she used both hands to fluff her hair back into shape.

"Maybe we ate too much ice cream in Chinquapin's," suggested Vickie, the sweet motherly figure who'd been the one to mistakenly grab Miz Eudora's arm.

"I think it's all the loot we bought in there," said Mary Beth, the woman who'd grabbed the other arm and was unaware of exactly how much loot she had carried on the bus. "Wasn't that just the most luscious little shop? I could look for days in places like that."

"Seems to me like you did look all day," scoffed Peggy, placing her hat in the bin overhead before she plopped in her seat.

"Now, Peggy, you know you enjoyed that store every bit as much as Mary Beth did," ribbed Rita, who was known for her bargain hunting.

"I know one thing. She surely spent as much as Mary Beth did," said Barbara, the woman who'd organized this trip.

"What's with you two?" asked Red Hat Nanny, known for her resolve. "We weren't here but thirty minutes."

"That's how come I love driving all you groups of Red Hat ladies around," stated the bus driver. "You women sure do know how to have a good time." He turned from the main road going through Hayesville onto the Highway 64 Bypass and headed toward Atlanta, the final destination on the women's mountain excursion from Winston Salem to Georgia. It was one of those "round your elbow" trips, but it hit all the places that Red Hatters from several state chapters had suggested for their combined fall touring event.

"Queen Angelbreeze, did you do a head count to make sure we didn't leave anyone back there?" asked Red Hat Nanny.

"I can answer that one," answered Barbara. "Queens don't have to handle such lowly jobs, but it sure seems to me we added a couple."

Peggy, the sailing expert of the bunch who

happened to be in the front seat, took over as captain and moved out into the aisle, counting heads aloud. "One, two, three, four, five,"

Her counting stopped as abruptly as the bus did when a van pulled out in front of them. When their driver hit the brakes, she hit the dashboard.

"Maybe you'd better sit down and count, lady," suggested the driver, making his apologies for her near miss of the windshield.

Peggy followed his advice and returned to her position on the front row behind the driver as she began to once again count. "One, two, three, four,"

"Oh, for goodness sake, Peggy. Can't you count up by twos?" asked Marlene.

"It comes from all those years of teaching," Vickie commiserated. "Most everyone on this bus is a former teacher so we all got used to counting with our students."

"Just let her count so that us 'Smokin' Babes' can get on with our game of rummy back here," called Barbara from the back seat.

"One, two, three, four, five…," Peggy started again, this time finishing with, "thirty-nine, forty, forty-one."

"You must have counted the driver, Peggy," stated Rita. "That's one too many."

"No, I'm sure I didn't." Peggy looked hard down the aisle, examining each seat to make sure no one had moved while she was counting. "I started with Mary Beth here in the front seat and saved myself for last."

"Okay, ladies," instructed Marlene, drawing on all her years' experience in the classroom, "all of you hold your red hats up in the air. Peggy will simply count the hats."

"One, two, three…," Peggy began once again, still ending with forty-one.

"Here, let me do it," called Barbara, who was getting antsy about finishing the rummy game that the women of her chapter had started before the stop in Hayesville.

It had been an unscheduled stop, but one the driver thought might appeal to the Red Hatters. Therefore, he'd taken a little side street to show them the quaint little courthouse of Clay County, North Carolina, and drive around its picturesque square. That had been when Mary Beth spotted the "cute little gift shop and general store" and Vickie saw "the ice cream bar" and the rummy game was halted.

All of the commotion now came to a halt as Miz Eudora stood from her seat. She started to speak, but stopped when everyone gasped, causing her to look out the front window to make sure another van hadn't pulled out in front of the bus.

"Where'd you come from?" shrieked Rita.

"Before or after I covered up Horace's casket?" Miz Eudora asked.

Heads turned abruptly to see if everyone had heard the same thing.

"You covered up a casket?" Peggy inquired, her words slow and tentative.

"Yes, but it was just my husband's," Miz Eudora answered, as if it were an everyday occurrence.

The rummy game no longer seemed a point of contention as the women wondered whether they had happened upon an axe murderer.

"Your...your husband's?" Vickie repeated cautiously.

"Yes, Horace's," Miz Eudora said. "We buried him today up on the mountain across the road from my house. I wanted to walk to Chinquapin's, but Sadie and Mabel insisted on taking me. Thank goodness, that sweet Sadie saw fit to take Mabel home before there was need for another burial."

The women glared at each other again.

"What did Horace die from?" ventured Marlene, not sure she wanted to know, but determined to make sure they weren't all going to be in the same boat as Mabel, whoever she was.

"Well, he sure didn't die from the same thing as John G. That had to be a horrible death," she said sympathetically, "having that thing stuck up your backside. But poor baby brother. I reckon compared to living with one of them Toasts, Mabel to beat, that was a blessing."

She looked at the women whose mouths were all gaped open. "He didn't die from tick fever, either." Getting no response, Miz Eudora continued, "Whatever it was from, Preacher Jake said it was a celebration. That's why I got so gussied up today before I helped bury Horace. Then I went to finish off the celebration with a cone of butter pecan ice cream down at Chinquapin's. That's when that nice young lady back there grabbed my arm and told me to "Come on," because the bus was leaving.

Heads turned as Vickie sank into her seat while pleading, "Look at her! She has on purple clothes and a red hat. How was I to know she wasn't one of us?"

"Vickie's always taking care of the poor and destitute," offered Mary Beth, trying to take up for her friend in front of the women from the other chapters.

"I told you we were more crowded than we'd been before that stop back there," insisted Marlene, making sure everyone was aware that she'd been correct in her presumption.

"You can let me out up here at the rusty mailbox beside the Scruggs' place," Miz Eudora volunteered, pointing up ahead. "I can walk over that ridge and get to my house from here. Thank you kindly for the ride. It was mighty nice of you to pick me up and give me a lift. This fopher coat sure is pretty, but it sure is hot after you been shoveling dirt. I'm deeply obliged."

Necks were craning to see the rusty mailbox and the ridge, and to make any sense of this strange woman who had mysteriously happened into their presence and was now causing such a disturbance.

Peggy, obviously not impressed with Miz Eudora's answers, again ascertained her position as captain by standing and taking a good look at the stranger. "Who are you? What are you doing and how did you get on this bus?"

The "poor and destitute" old woman looked as if she might cry as the bus kept going and missed her stop at the Scruggs' place.

Red Hat Nanny, the acclaimed "Nanny" of the group – even to the point of having it in her royal title – came forward. "Ladies," she reminded politely, "where are your red hat Southern manners?"

She put a reassuring hand on Miz Eudora's arm, which was now clinched in fright as she held tightly to her red leather purse. "My name is Peggy, but since there are two of us by that name in this group, they call me Red Hat Nanny. I'm from South Carolina and I belong to four Red Hat chapters. Seems I just can't get enough of these crazy ladies."

Peggy motioned a hand back, drawing Miz Eudora's eyes to the many heads on the bus. "I make red hats. Some of these women have on one of my creations." She offered a beautiful smile. "I love my grandchildren. That's why they call me the Red Hat Nanny."

"She even has a red PT Cruiser to tool around in," added Rita.

Miz Eudora felt a twinge of comforting consolation in the sweetness of Red Hat Nanny's voice that reminded her of Sadie. She thought of their afternoon chats and was able to get past the approaching tears of uncertainty of all the events of the past few days. A smile finally graced her lips as she said, "My name is Eudora. Eudora Rumph. People who know me just call me Miz Eudora." Feeling a bit safer now, her smile grew. "That's so much more pleasant sounding than Eudora Rumph."

Peggy sensed a few snickers behind her as the Red Hatters began to loosen up, too. "Then we'll call you Miz Eudora. How's that?"

"That'll be fine," Miz Eudora replied with a nod. "I live in Smackass Gap, just back up the road from where you were in Hayesville."

Apparently even the gift of grandchildren had not prepared the Red Hat Nanny for that remark, for she stood boggled.

"Did you say 'Smackass Gap?'" asked Mary Beth as a tiny ripple of laughter began in a wave fashion around the bus, spreading even to the driver.

"I sure did," Miz Eudora answered proudly. "It's pretty close after you passed the turn off for Shooting Creek. I live on Downings Creek Road, right past where you turn on Jarrett Road."

"You said you live in a place called Smackass Gap?" Marlene asked, as if perhaps she'd been mistaken in her hearing.

"Yep! It starts there about where you saw the water for Lake Chatuge."

"And you actually *call* it Smackass Gap?" inquired Vickie.

"What else would we call it?" came the rhetorical question. "Where do you live?" she asked Vickie.

"In New Bern, North Carolina," Vickie answered.

"And what do you call it?" Miz Eudora asked

courteously.

"We call it New Bern," Vickie confirmed, receiving nods from all the other ladies on the bus who also lived in New Bern.

"Well, see there?" Miz Eudora pointed out quite matter-of-factly. "We all live somewhere and we all call it by its name. Now that we got that straight, there's another house up here where I can get off and walk across the ridge." She took a handkerchief out of her purse and waved it, as a signal for the driver, and as a good-bye to the women.

"How do you spell Smackass Gap?" Rita asked.

"Just like it says on the sign down at the bottom of Chunky Gal Mountain," came the answer.

"Wait a minute," Barbara requested, trying to get past the name of Miz Eudora's hometown. "I want to make sure I understand. You said you buried your husband just today?"

"That's right," Miz Eudora affirmed. "Just a couple of hours ago. He's laid to rest right beside his pa and ma and the three little ones his ma lost in childbirth. Some of the rest of his family is scattered around the cemetery with the families they married into." Miz Eudora offered a winsome smile. "I put the last shovel of dirt on him myself. I thought that would be a nice final gesture."

"You buried your husband in that?" Marlene asked, appalled that this woman would have worn such an outfit to a memorial service.

"Oh, no! I handed my purple fopher coat to Sadie while I covered him up. She held it for me until the pallbearers and I finished."

There was a moment of stunned silence as Miz Eudora turned back to Red Hat Nanny. "I don't have any children, so therefore, I don't have any grandchildren. I don't make red hats, but I sure can make some mean leather britches. They win at the county fair every year alongside of my hominy."

Miz Eudora wiped the sweat from her brow onto the handkerchief. "I don't have a red cruiser, but Horace had a red Massey-Ferguson, and seeing as how he's gone now, I reckon as to how it's mine. It occasionally pops out of second gear, but the rest of the gears work fine enough to 'tool around' the field on."

She waved to Mary Beth. "Thank you for helping me get up into this bus. I've not ever been in such a fine vehicle before. I even heard one of the ladies say it had a bathroom. Land's sakes, I didn't even know you could get indoor plumbing in these things."

Seeing that they had indeed happened upon a

rare treasure, the women began to ask all sorts of questions about mountain life and the culture of Miz Eudora.

"There ain't nothing cultured on the farm except buttermilk and Horace's special blend, but then, we don't talk about that, especially now that he's gone."

"I'd never given a thought to wearing my red hat to a memorial service," stated Peggy.

"Me, neither," replied Miz Eudora. "I had all intentions of hunting my black wool dress out of the cedar chest, even though I was sure it was covered in moth holes. But Preacher Jake insisted that Horace's funeral was a celebration. I never was so shocked to learn that everybody in Smackass Gap was so glad to learn about his passing. They come bearing food like you ain't ever seen. He must have really made a lot of people mad with his special blend. I reckon he stole a lot of business around the county."

"So how did you find out about red hats?" asked Red Hat Nanny.

"P'SHAA!" exclaimed Miz Eudora. "There wasn't nothing to it. After Preacher Jake told me about the celebration, I figured I needed something party-like to wear since all my lightweight flour sack dresses had short sleeves. I decided Horace didn't get up that morning with the intention of passing the Jordan, so it was okay. It was God's way of letting me get a new dress. You know, it had only been a little over twenty years since I got the last one, but since it was a celebration, I figured as to what I could splurge a little. Especially since Horace wasn't around to complain about it.

"I had to pay for the rest of this outfit, but this hat, it was a blessing from God. You know, they say what goes around comes around. I've always been good to share my bountiful garden harvests with others, so I reckon that's how this hat came to me. It was just laying by itself in the back room of the thrift store where the sign said everything was free. It must have went around from somebody else and landed there and I come around and picked it up. On my way out the door, I happened to see this little piece of purple plume on the floor, so I picked it up and stuck it on the hat."

Miz Eudora adjusted the hat. "It adds a nice little touch, don't you think?"

Red Hat Nanny laughed. "Yes, I do think!"

"I wasn't too sure about wearing red at first." Miz Eudora leaned forward to make sure the bus driver couldn't hear her. "I didn't know much of anything about red besides what I'd heard of red lights, and I knew I didn't want no part of that. But since all you nice, kind ladies are wearing red hats, I reckon it's all right to be seen in a red hat. I sure didn't want anybody thinking the wrong thing about me. Especially since I had this red purse and shoes, too."

Snickers and comments abounded as Queen Angelbreeze and Red Hat Nanny told Miz Eudora all about the red hats and how they got started.

"What's the name of your chapter?" asked Marlene.

"Huh?" asked Eudora.

"Your chapter?" repeated Marlene. "What chapter do you belong to?"

"I don't know nothing about a chapter, but my class is on the book of Leviticus."

"No, Miz Eudora," explained Mary Beth.

"Your chapter is part of an organization."

"Oh, you mean like my quilters and the Maiden's Maidens?" she asked, beginning to understand.

"Yes," replied Vickie.

"For instance," Queen Angelbreeze went on to explain, "we're members of the Hot G.R.I.T.S. and Red Hats. Hold up your hands back there," she instructed as she gave a confident beam. "I'm the queen of our chapter."

Barbara waved her handful of cards from the

back row and said, "I'm one of the Smokin' Babes."

"And I belong to the Red Hat Floosies," added Red Hat Nanny.

"I got it," Miz Eudora responded with a nod. "Well, I guess you could say I'm a member of the Livermush and Red Aprons." Miz Eudora smiled as all the ladies on the van laughed. "You ladies are welcome to come up and be a member of my chapter anytime you want."

By the time the women on the bus had sufficiently learned all about Miz Eudora Rumph and Smackass Gap, Peggy yelled up at the driver. "Excuse me, sir. We need to get this lady back home. Could we stop somewhere and turn around?"

"Not unless you ladies want to haul buggy from Atlanta. You've all been back there jabbering so long that we're only one block from the restaurant where you're scheduled to stop for dinner."

A forlorn expression again settled on Miz Eudora's face.

"What's the matter?" asked Red Hat Nanny, seeing the pained look.

"I didn't bring a lick of money with me," admitted Miz Eudora. "Seeing as how they weren't going to take up an offering at Horace's funeral, I didn't see any need. Rob wouldn't let me pay for the cone of ice cream on account of me being such a new widow and I never thought about supper. We had enough food in my kitchen for the whole county."

"Don't worry about that, Miz Eudora," offered Vickie. "I'll spot you for dinner."

The size of Miz Eudora's eyes doubled. "Spot me? On my brand new old clothes?"

"That's just an expression, dear," consoled Mary Beth. "It means she'll pay for yours since you don't have your wallet. She's always the one to take care of…," She caught herself before uttering the next words.

"Special friends," said Marlene. "She's always the one to take care of our special friends since she's the treasurer for our chapter."

"I'll pay you as soon as I get home," Miz Eudora assured them.

"No need for that, either," declared Peggy. "This is our way of showing our sympathy."

"My goodness," said Miz Eudora. "Everyone's being so nice. I reckon Preacher Jake was right when he said Horace's passing was a celebration. Since everybody's being so generous, it's too bad he didn't take up a collection."

AFTER I CURTLY dropped Mabel off at the motel,

I took the liberty of driving back to the church, parking the car and walking up the hill to the freshly dug grave. Miz Eudora had hinted on the way to the church that morning that she wanted to walk home from the cemetery alone. I had strongly protested, but finally I gave in to her whim, realizing that she was old enough and wise enough to best decide how she wanted to deal with her grief.

Now, as I stood there reliving my own loss, I replayed our morning's conversation in my mind. "Are you sure you won't let me drive you back home, Miz Eudora?" I asked. "I'll wait until after everyone has paid their final respects and spoken their words of condolence to you."

There had been something horrid about the mental image I'd had of this poor woman left alone at the cemetery to walk home. That's why I was secretly thrilled for the opportunity to take her to Chinquapin's for ice cream, even though it had come at the insistence of Mabel.

As I looked from the cemetery down the hill to my house, and then on across Highway 64 to her house far across the way, I could still hear her words ringing in my ear. "Sadie, I've walked home with Horace many a time from this cemetery," she had assured me.

"Yes," I had replied, "but he's not going home

with you this time." The moment I had uttered those words, their reality struck me. I prayed she'd not noticed that I'd taken a big chunk off the proverbial foot that I'd placed in my mouth.

She obviously didn't, for she continued with, "Just because his body is going to be laying six feet under don't mean the memory of Horace Rumph is not going to go with me everywhere I go."

I had stared at her in disbelief. *First my husband and now this woman*, I thought, fully absorbing her prophetic words of wisdom and counsel. Visions of Loretta's last visit also flashed before me as I imagined her saying those same words to me, which I'm sure she would have heard Leon saying to someone else.

Sadie Calloway, you need to go home and take Leon's memories with you and leave Eudora Rumph to deal with the loss of her own husband in her own way. I'd heard those words this morning and I heard them again now. They were so plainly distinguishable in my mind's ear, they might as well have been uttered by Leon himself.

I stood there, I guess in prayer, but not really sure how to pray, before slowly driving down the hill from the cemetery. While glancing back in my mirror at the dirt pile, I continued, in my small way, to pray for Miz Eudora, *and myself*, to find peace.

May her celebration continue, I pleaded, hoping God would listen to the petition of a person who'd not been in the habit of calling on Him.

WHEN THE PHONE rang early the next morning, I wondered who it could be. *It surely isn't Miz Eudora*, I reminded myself, *for she has no phone.* As I pulled the receiver close to my ear, I could already hear Mabel squawking from the other end.

"Well, now you've gone and done it, Sadie Callaway," she grumbled.

"Done what?" I asked, completely clueless.

"Let something horrible happen to Eudora," she answered more curtly than I'd been when I dropped her off the afternoon before.

I rubbed my eyes, as if that would help me hear better. "What happened? What's horrible?"

"She's not at home. I went there this morning to tell her that I'd decided to move here and she wasn't there."

Maybe she had a warning dream, I wanted to say. *If I'd been in her shoes and had an inkling of you making that announcement, I'd have been gone, too.* But rather than state that to her, I replied politely, "I'm sure she walked to the cemetery."

"Oh, no, she didn't!" Mabel stormed. "I went

there thinking the same thing."

Somehow, the notion of Mabel and I thinking the same thing was not very comforting.

"I'll get dressed and meet you at her house," I suggested. As I threw on some clothes suitable for taking a hike through the fields in search of her, my mind began to form its own images of all the things that could have happened once we'd left her at Chinquapin's.

That's it! I resolved, picking up the phone to dial Rob Tiger. I was sure he wouldn't mind the early call considering the situation.

"Nope," he said. "Sorry. I didn't see anything out of the ordinary. There was a bus filled with Red Hatters that pulled into the town square shortly after you got the ice cream, but they were only there about thirty minutes. Last time I saw her, she was still sitting on the bench enjoying her cone."

"Thanks!" I offered, while looking up the number for The Fam. "Maybe she got a 'hankering' to have breakfast out since she's never done that before," I said aloud while dialing Tommy.

"Nope, haven't seen her," he answered. "And believe me, if that woman would have come in for breakfast, everyone would have noticed. I dare say she's never eaten breakfast away from her own kitchen table."

I hung up and headed as hard as I could in the car across Highway 64 onto Downings Creek Road. I'd walked through nearly all the barns when Rob's statement surfaced in my mind.

A bus filled with Red Hatters. I stopped in place. *No, it couldn't be. They'd have noticed her by now.* I gave a big sigh and walked back toward the front porch where I'd left Mabel to give a big yell should Miz Eudora show up. I contemplated whether to tell her about my hunch, but before I had the chance, Sheriff Bonner pulled into the Rumph driveway.

"Morning, ladies," he greeted us. Then he handed me a piece of paper. "When I didn't see your car at home, I thought you might be here. Got a message for you."

"Oh, dear!" screamed Mabel. "What's happened? Somebody call Preacher Jake. I'd better get started writing her obituary."

"Cut the crap!" I ordered, repeating what I'd heard Miz Eudora say to her the day before, which seemed to be the only three words that would shut her up. "First of all, nothing's happened. Miz Eudora is just fine and having a grand old time. And second of all, even if she weren't, you wouldn't be writing her obituary. I wouldn't want her turning over in her grave."

My first reaction was that I wanted to jump up and down in triumph at putting Mabel in her place. ***Too bad you can't put her some place besides Smackass Gap!*** I told myself, quickly dissipating my air of victory. My second reaction was that I hated Leon wasn't here to see my "I am woman. Hear me roar!" attitude.

"Humph!" Mabel rattled

"Thanks, Sheriff Bonner. I'll leave right now and be in Atlanta within two hours."

"I'm going with you," Mabel declared, opening the passenger door of my Taurus.

Any other time I would have argued, but I figured she'd simply climb in her Buick and follow me. With that thought, I reached out my hand. "Give me your keys. We're taking your car," I said.

"What?" she asked indignantly.

"You heard me. Hand them over. I'm going to make sure Miz Eudora rides back in comfort. She's had an eventful night."

I left Mabel to quietly stew and wonder about the events of the night as I took off toward my old stomping ground of Atlanta and the downtown Wyndham Garden Hotel.

"HOW IN THE world did you get picked up by a

bus load of Red Hatters?" fumed Mabel as we sat inside the lobby of the luxurious hotel where Miz Eudora had spent her first evening alone in her whole life.

Of course she wasn't really alone. She had been befriended by forty other Red Hatters and one admiring bus driver. I noticed that during the ranting and raving, Mabel was taking careful note of the place that was probably nicer than any place she'd ever occupied.

"Even for you, Eudora Rumph, that's hard to believe," Mabel continued.

"Well…,"

There's that word, I thought, pulling up the plush, winged chair and willing my ears to full attention. *A good story is on the way*, I anticipated, sensing Mabel would not be as humored as I by what was to follow.

"I was sitting on the bench of the sidewalk in front of Chinquapin's, taking one last lick of my butter pecan ice cream, before starting on the cone. All of a sudden, some woman, who I later learned was Vickie," she said, giving a big wave toward the woman I presumed to be her, "grabbed my arm. 'C'mon,' she said, 'you don't want to miss the bus.'

"She acted like she knew me and then Mary Beth grabbed the other arm. I felt so bad for her, because she didn't get any ice cream, that I started to give her my cone. But since the cone was Horace's favorite part, I ate it in memory of him since it was his celebration." Miz Eudora paused and waved at the woman who must have been Mary Beth.

"For all I knew, they were some of those people what was so glad to learn about Horace's passing that they'd come to join in the grand finale of the big celebration. Land's sakes, for all I knew, we were going to that nice big Community Center over in Brasstown for watermelon." She turned to me with a huge grin. "Sadie, that bus was the nicest thing. It even had indoor plumbing."

I smiled and wished that I could have been there to celebrate the grand finale with her. One thing was for sure. I was definitely going to be present when she informed Preacher Jake what a glorious celebration it had been.

"Anyway," continued Miz Eudora, "all those women were dressed in their festive red hats, too, and they all acted like they knew me. At least, until they started counting and had an extra hat. It took them a few minutes to realize that I didn't murder Horace before I buried him. But then once we all got used to each other and I knew they weren't going to hurt me, we got to swapping stories and having such a good time that I didn't even realize we'd crossed the state line and was headed for 'Hotlanta.'"

I laughed, knowing she had truly had a Red Hat "night on the town" if she knew to call it "Hotlanta."

"How could you not know you'd crossed the state line?" Mabel scoffed, sounding more grateful to have the opportunity to grill her sister-in-law than concerned about her disappearance.

"Honey," Barbara shot at Mabel, "had you been on that bus with us, you'd have seen how she could have not known that."

"Yeah," piped up Vickie, "you've obviously never been introduced to the good times us women in red hats have."

A sea of forty red hats and one blue bus driver's hat nodded in agreement.

"Just think, we got ourselves a stowaway," announced Rita. "Wait until we tell the women back home. They'll be so jealous that they didn't come."

"Stowaway, my foot!" accused Mabel. "You took this poor, defenseless soul across state lines without her knowledge or written consent. That seems liable for charges, if you ask me. Kidnapping in the first degree, if I ever heard it."

"Kidnapping?" reeled Red Hat Nanny. "Oh dear, do you think they could arrest us for this?"

I wanted to laugh at the cacophony of responses. They could have very well been a spoken antiphonal choir on the Lincoln Center stage rather than a group of red-topped tourists as forty-two voices, including Miz Eudora's and the bus driver's joined the ruckus.

"Oh, wouldn't that be a hoot?" laughed Peggy. "A raid on the charter bus of a bunch of ladies over fifty! That would be such a headline that none of our members would ever want to miss another trip."

"You got that right," agreed Barbara, getting high fives from the Smokin' Babes.

The sea of hats, red and blue, was in motion again.

"Ladies," came Queen Angelbreeze's voice, demanding crowd control, "it would appear that we did actually cross a state line with Miz Eudora. This could be a fairly serious offense."

"Nonsense!" roared Peggy. "She wasn't an unwilling soul."

"She wasn't willing, either," Mary Beth reminded them. "We simply shoved her on the bus, thinking she was one of us. I don't think anyone gave her a choice."

"Why didn't she say something if she wasn't one of us?" asked Rita.

Miz Eudora turned to me again, her voice

nearly as shaky as the morning when she'd found Horace's lifeless body. "Sadie, these women came to 'Hotlanta' to 'have a hot time in the old town tonight.' I sure do hope I didn't make them miss their hot time."

"Oh, Miz Eudora," said Vickie, whose voice broke into tears.

"Honey," continued Red Hat Nanny, "being with you was a hotter time than anything we could have gotten ourselves into in Hotlanta. If you ask me, you're one hot Red Hat dame just waiting to explode."

Miz Eudora's face looked a bit puzzled.

"She's paying you a great compliment," I explained to her quietly. "Just say 'Thank You.'"

"Thank you," Miz Eudora nodded, her voice trailing off. "I think." She turned to me. "I wasn't even upset, much less mad," she explained, wondering why they thought she was "just waiting to explode."

"No, Miz Eudora, they know that," I assured her. "All they meant was they think you're about the most fun person they've ever met. It's simply their way of saying that, like when you say something in a way I don't understand."

"She's right," confirmed Rita. "You're just about the wildest thing I've ever seen."

"She's wild, all right," said Mabel. "C'mon," she added, taking her sister-in-law's arm. "It's time to take you home."

"You're not taking me anywhere," Miz Eudora replied, jerking her arm away. "Why, I wouldn't ride in that Buick of yours for nothing."

"I'll have you know I'm a good driver," Mabel informed her.

"It's not your driving I don't like," crowed Miz Eudora. "It's you."

I saw that if we didn't soon leave, the Red Hatters might get their chance to see their "one hot Red Hat dame" explode for sure. "She's not driving, I am," I quickly said. "And I'm going to show you my old house while we're in downtown Atlanta. You're in my back yard now."

"That's more like it," she replied, following me toward the door. "Do you think we can drop Mabel off somewhere on the way?"

I didn't dare tell her that Mabel was planning a move to Smackass Gap. That would surely blow her top.

All forty of the women ran to the door to give Miz Eudora a hug. Even the bus driver had a tear in his eye as he gave her a solid shake of the hand. "You're about the most entertaining passenger I ever did have, Miz Eudora. You come back and travel with Peacock Bus Lines anytime."

"Thank you," she acknowledged. "You all sure did end Horace's celebration with a bang. If I'd have known you were coming through Hayesville, we'd have held the service later so you could have been there. Preacher Jake surely did do a nice job with it." She stopped once more as she reached the lobby's exit and turned around. Waving her handkerchief, she added, "I sure do hope I get to see you all again."

"Sure thing!" yelled Queen Angelbreeze. "I'll let Sadie know when we're having our meetings and events. Maybe ya'll can come join us."

Miz Eudora's face broke into the biggest grin I'd ever seen on her. "Sure thing!"

That's how it was that I came to learn that when Miz Eudora did something, she did it with gusto…and a red hat!

NINE

A Crow's Feet

SEEING AS HOW I'd taken on the newly self-assumed responsibility of making sure Miz Eudora turned a new leaf on life, I thought as how a trip to the grocery store was in order after her experience with the Red Hatters. ***Not to mention the news of Mabel staying in Smackass Gap***, which nearly did make the Buick a convertible, or at least a sunroof. I stopped at Miz Eudora's house long enough to get my car and rid ourselves of Mabel. Then I informed the bereaved that we had one more item of business to attend to before the celebration came to a close.

"Land's sakes!" she exclaimed as expected, right on cue, as I pulled into the parking lot of the Ingle's grocery store on Highway 64. "I'll bet there's enough food in that place to feed everybody in the western half of North Carolina." She eyed the façade carefully as I parked the car. "And maybe even some of the eastern half." The woman did have a point, seeing as how this was the only actual "supermarket" in town, and it stood next to the corner with the one stoplight in Hayesville – that is, until they recently got their second stoplight.

I chuckled as I asked, "Have you never been here, Miz Eudora?"

"Why on earth would I need to come here?" she asked back. "This place is so big that I'll bet a body could get lost in there."

We'd already lost her body one time in the past two days; I wasn't interested in an instant reply. As harmless as a trip to the supermarket seemed, though, my "Eudoradar" (short for Eudora radar) told me this was going to be an event to remember.

The more I thought about it, she probably didn't have a need for Ingle's. She raised her own livestock, vegetables and fruit. Her corn meal was freshly ground. For all I knew, she probably had sugar cane somewhere on her large expanse of property. She'd grown up in an era when all the area farmers went into the square of Hayesville on Saturday mornings, their truck beds loaded with produce, and parked them in front of what was then the general store.

Definitely* not *like most of the kids in

Atlanta who think that ground beef comes from the corner grocery chain! I couldn't help but think.

"So you've never been to a grocery store?" I asked.

"Oh, I've been to a grocery store, all right," she informed me. "Back in the forties, Tiger's Cash Store stood where Chinquapin's is now. Why, that was a regular supermarket back in those days. Granted, it had dry goods on the side of the store where the ice cream parlor and collectibles are now, but the entire other side was groceries, most of which was produce. I can remember Papa taking bushels of squash, half-runners, corn, and watermelons, whatever we had growing at the time, and Tiger's Cash Store would buy it from him to sell in the grocery store.

"People didn't have nothing back then, so Mr. Tiger was good to take chickens in exchange for basic commodities. Otherwise, some folks in the county wouldn't have made it. They was all still hurting from the depression."

She nodded her head as I caught a glimpse of a fond memory forming across her forehead. "Yep, that Tiger family has always been good to the people of Clay County. I guess that's why when I didn't know what to do with myself yesterday after Horace's service, I felt safe in heading over to

Rob's. They're good stock, that family."

Miz Eudora looked at me as if she'd just exited a wonderful thought bubble. "But if you're asking me if I've ever been in a *real* supermarket since Tiger's Cash Store, the answer is no." She shook her head as if the act of avoiding a chain grocer were a great accomplishment. From the way she said it, I felt like I was taking her to some forbidden place where your mother might have warned you against going. My gut feeling, though, encouraged me to trust my "Eudoradar" and march her right into the Ingle's.

Even if it does seem anticlimactic on the heels of her adventure with the Red Hatters! I tried to convince myself.

I'd considered dropping her off at the front door, just to be sure she didn't get "lost" for a second time. However, given her "festive celebration clothes" and the lack of a sea of red hats in the Ingle's parking lot, I felt pretty confident that she'd not "go missing" a second time.

From her first step inside the door, she looked bug-eyed, much the same way as when I'd answered the door to see Milton T. Toast at her door a couple of days earlier. *Talk about a kid in a candy store*, I mused as I watched her walk down one aisle and then the other. *Or should I say, "culture shock?"* I wondered.

I went about getting my groceries, peering around corners to keep an eye on her, while she "took in" lots of new things for the first time. I'd barely made it past the pickle aisle, which was no longer a necessary stop for me since Miz Eudora kept me in bread-and-butter and dill pickles from her canning shed, when I heard my name.

"Sadie! Oh, Sadie-e-e, where are you? You've got to see this."

I pushed my cart as fast as I could toward the direction of the announcement, but in a roundabout way so that hopefully too many people wouldn't notice that I was the person being "paged."

"Look at this!" she ordered when I turned the corner toward her, still in a voice that could be heard all over the supermarket. "They got food in here I can't even pronounce. I'm sure not going to eat something if I can't say what it is."

I heard several giggles from throughout the store. In a hushed tone, I explained to her that some people used the items for Mexican, Italian or other ethnic recipes.

"What's wrong with American food?" she asked. I saw in her eyes that the question was purely innocent and she really didn't know that food of other cultures had become so popular, or that there was such an influx of nationalities to the area. Standing there and watching her, I seriously doubted that she'd ever had spaghetti and I was sure she'd never tasted a taco. I didn't think this was the time to be introducing her to a new cuisine, so I suggested she try the back of the store where milk, eggs and bacon were located.

I left her and went back to my shopping, hoping for no more "incidents" of having my name called. All seemed to be fine until I'd gone down a couple more aisles. I looked back to see her at the packaged lunchmeat counter, standing beside a woman also wearing a red hat. The woman was dressed in a purple skirt, a red-and-purple striped blouse, red pumps and a purple crocheted shawl. Immediately, I glanced in every direction to make sure we'd not happened upon another group of Red Hatters. I had no intention of "losing a body" in the Ingle's store.

Trying my best to stay out of their view, I inched my way back to where I could keep an eye on them. So as not to appear too conspicuous to passing customers, I took cans off the shelf, inspected them and put them back – all while keeping my "stake-out" post on the soup aisle. It was a strain, but I managed to eavesdrop on their conversation.

"Did your husband die, too?" I heard Miz

Eudora asked compassionately.

Why'd she ask that? I wondered, listening more intently.

"Yes, but he's been dead a long time," the woman answered.

"And I thought Horace's death was a celebration! You must have had a lot to celebrate to still be dressed like that."

I tried to keep my snicker silent as I detected the course for which the conversation was headed. Now I understood Miz Eudora's question.

"What do you mean?" asked the woman, who looked a bit startled at this interest in her husband's passing.

"Well," Miz Eudora began, "Preacher Jake told me not to wear my black mourning dress to my late husband's funeral. He said it was a celebration, so that's why I've got on these bright colors. I wanted to be dressed for the occasion. Since your clothes are the very same colors, I figured you lost your man, too."

"When did your husband die?" the woman questioned.

"Three days ago," replied Miz Eudora. "I'm on my home from his funeral now.

"I'm sorry to hear that," came a sympathetic response. "That's really sad."

"Oh, don't be sorry." Miz Eudora pulled out a tissue and handed it to Hattie, who wiped her eyes. "It's not sad at all. Everybody around Smackass Gap's been partying since he passed. Or at least since Preacher Jake declared it a celebration. There's been more food at my house than the church has had at Homecoming for the past three years put together." She looked around at all the aisles laden with food. "There's so much food, it might could even make a dent in this here place."

Miz Eudora adjusted her hat. "And I like these clothes so much, I believe I'll do like you and keep on celebrating. People do seem to stand up and take notice when I walk in the room now. They didn't ever pay much attention to my flour sack dresses."

"I'm surprised you even felt like coming to the grocery store," commented the woman. "When my husband died, all I wanted to do at first was sit in the house and be alone with the spirit of his presence."

"Well, I was really on my way home yesterday, and I guess you could say that I wanted to be alone. Except I didn't want to be alone with the spirit of Horace's presence. I don't get into Horace's spirits. They're way too strong for my liking. That's why I reckon I wanted to be alone with an ice cream cone from Chinquapin's. There was lots of memories at Tiger's, most of them which didn't include Horace, but they were all happy memories."

I could tell from the expression on the woman's face that she had no clue what Miz Eudora was babbling about.

"That's when these nice ladies in red hats took me on a little 'excursion,' they called it," Miz Eudora went on. They even 'spotted' my supper, but I'm still not sure what that means. All I know is that we had purple mashed potatoes, but they called them Peruvian Blue smashed potatoes. I never saw anything like them and I been eatin' taters all my life! I reckon they're like my "fopher" coat. The color might be a little odd, but they sure were pretty. They tasted real good, too. Like they had lots of fresh churned butter in them."

I watched as the woman picked up a plastic container of pimento cheese, which I assumed was so she could get on with her life and away from all of Miz Eudora's ramblings.

"They were real nice, but they took me across the Georgia state line, so then Sadie and Mabel had to come and get me. We dropped Mabel off and now we're going home as soon as Sadie gets done shopping."

"I see," replied the woman as she stuck her

finger under the lid of the pimento cheese and took a little taste.

Miz Eudora must have been hungry, for she followed suit and before I could stop her, she had her finger in another container of pimento cheese.

"What are you doing?" I yelled, trying not to startle Miz Eudora, but stop her before she got us kicked out of Ingle's. Given it was the "only ballgame in town," I would have nowhere else to shop without going to Franklin or crossing the state line if she got us ejected from the establishment.

"I'm tasting the food," Miz Eudora answered with all innocence of a three-year-old, reminding me of my earlier thought about the kid in the candy store. *Or culture shock.* The only problem was, I still wasn't sure which of the two cases it was.

"You don't expect us to pay for this if it isn't any good, do you?" challenged the other woman with the red hat. "And how else are we going to know whether it's any good?"

The woman had a point. They grew up in the days where you would not have bought 'a pig in a poke.' The problem was, I had no clue of how to explain modern shopping protocol to them, seeing as how they were both several years my senior. I looked into her bright blue eyes, full of life, and saw the framing of an intense personality. She was a short woman, but I could tell from her demeanor that what she was lacking in height, she wasn't lacking in spunk.

I reached out and took both containers of pimento cheese. "Here, why don't we put these in my buggy? I suddenly have a craving for pimento cheese."

"Wait!" called the woman as she reached for another brand. "There might be one here that tastes better."

"That's quite all right," I hastily replied. "These two will do very well for what I need." *And what I need is to pay for these and throw them away*, I reasoned in my attempt to get us out of the store with as little attention as necessary.

As I eyed the pair in front of me, I first feared we might need a diversion to get us out of Ingle's. But then my eyes discovered something else as I stared at them. For I beheld two souls, probably only a few years apart in age, who had seen more in life than I'd ever dream about. They'd lived through the Great Depression, the Great War…and from the look of things, a great time of taking care of themselves and others around them. I decided I didn't need to explain anything to them, but bask in the wealth of their combined experiences and knowledge.

I also decided I needed to hotfoot it down to the Christian Love Ministries Store and look for my own purple outfit and red hat. I was missing out on a lot of celebrating.

Reaching a hand out to the unknown woman, I said, "I don't believe we've been properly introduced. My name is Sadie Calloway, and this is my dear friend Eudora Rumph, but everyone who knows her calls her Miz Eudora."

A radiant smile fell on her face. "How do you do, Sadie?" Her warm, hazel eyes moved to Miz Eudora. "And I guess I know you well enough to call you Miz Eudora since we've shared pimento cheese together."

I wasn't sure about Miz Eudora, but I could tell that I adored this woman already.

"My name is Hattie Crow. C-R-O-W, just like the bird. I just recently moved here from Hickory. I'm still trying to get to know the area."

If she gets to know Clay County like she gets to know pimento cheese, she'll know it better than me, or even Miz Eudora, soon. I gave a little chuckle as I realized that was exactly how Miz Eudora had gotten to know everything in life. She'd sampled it. She'd opened it up and had a little taste. And if she didn't like it, she closed it back and had nothing to do with it. *There's something to that*

philosophy, I determined, also determining to give
their way of thinking a try.

"Hickory?" asked Miz Eudora. "That's where
my… this person I know grew up. Did you live
there long?"

"All my life," Hattie answered, beaming.
"What's this person's name?"

"Her name is Mabel Jarvis, but she was
Mabel Toast back then."

"Mabel Toast?" Hattie screeched in
recognition of the name. "Did she have a sister
named Melba and a brother named Milton T?"

Miz Eudora nodded in disbelief that this
woman knew the triplets.

"Why, they were in my class growing up all
the way through school. Their grandparents lived
just down the road from my grandparents, who lived
on the corner at Lenoir-Rhyne, the Lutheran college
there. My family were all good Lutherans. In fact,
the Miller's Lutheran Church in Hickory was named
after my great-grandfather because he gave them
the land. But there's a lot of Lutheran churches there.
I know one place where you can stand and see seven
different Lutheran churches."

"You actually had to watch them beady-eyed
young'uns growing up?" Miz Eudora asked in shock.
"No wonder you're so short. That was enough to

stunt your growth."

"I did more than watch them. Because our grandparents lived so close together, I had to play with them. 'The three little toasts,' we called them."

So I see I was not the first person to think of them that way! I mused.

"I liked to play with Melba and Milton T. Melba was always a sweet girl. We called her 'Buttered Toast' because she was like sweet home-churned butter, plain but good. Milton T. was called 'Strawberry Jam on Toast' because he was so colorful. If that had been today, a few people might have wondered about him. But that Mabel, we all called her 'Burnt Toast' because she was always such a sourpuss and tried to tell the rest of us what to do and how to do it.

Before my thought on the matter had time to cross my brain, Miz Eudora said it aloud. "Some things never change. Those three are still just like that and that Mabel is still burnt. She was pretty fired up when she left my house two days ago, and she wasn't much better when we dropped her off a little bit ago at the motel where she stayed during the funeral and all."

"She's here?" Hattie asked. "Mabel Toast is here in Clay County?"

"Yep. Just down the road at the Deerfield Inn.

Except she's a Jarvis now. She was married to my baby brother, John G., poor thing, but he died. Being around that Mabel for very long is enough to kill anybody off!"

Hattie laughed. "Too bad he couldn't have sampled her like the pimento cheese first!"

Now that's the best thought I've heard in a long time, I decided as I watched the two of them. They had already formed a bond, a sisterhood, standing right in the middle of the lunchmeat counter. What I'd picked up there reminded me of the makings of a Ray Stevens' song rather than a sandwich. *I knew this grocery store visit was going to be a memorable event!* my subconscious reminded me.

"I'd better get going. I walked down here and walking back is harder. Down the mountain isn't so bad, but my knees grumble when they start up the hill."

"Why don't you let Sadie take you home?" asked Miz Eudora. "I'm sure she wouldn't mind, would you, Sadie?" she suggested, turning to me.

"No, not at all," I gladly offered. Being around these two was the best medicine I'd had in ages. The funny thing was, I didn't even know I needed medicine until after I'd listened to the two of them for five minutes.

"Thank you," replied Hattie, "but I have an appointment with the pedicurist before I can go home."

"Oh, my!" exclaimed Miz Eudora. "Is that anything like a proctologist? John G. was one of them and that's what finally did him in. You might better be careful going to one of them," she earnestly warned.

I couldn't hold in the laugh, which I feared was as loud as her call for me had been.

"Miz Eudora, I'm going to get a pedicure on my feet," Hattie explained, also laughing. "It won't do me in, but I surely won't go to sleep while I'm in the chair. I went to sleep in the beautician's chair last week and that's what happened to my hair," she said, pulling on the short strands of hair that were left. "My cat's got longer hair than me now."

"How could you fall asleep when someone has scissors on your head?" Miz Eudora asked incredulously.

"I always take a nap in the beautician's chair," answered Hattie.

"I guess I see your point," replied Miz Eudora. "Whatever a pedicurist is, you wouldn't want him to cut your feet off."

My laugh grew louder, as did Hattie's.

"No worry of that," Hattie replied. "Why

don't you two ride there with me? Then you can take me home. I've already cooked a big supper and you can be my guests."

"We've got plenty of food at my place," said Miz Eudora, "but I'd like to have supper with you. Then you can come to my place for dinner tomorrow. We can even invite Mabel if you want to, so you can see that she's like she always was. That ought to get her goat good when she sees I met someone who knew her back then." She looked at me. "Is that all right with you, Sadie?"

"It sounds like a plan to me!" I answered, paying for only the items I had in my cart and leaving the rest of my needs for another time.

Once we got in the car, Hattie explained that a pedicurist works with nails.

"Land's sakes!" Miz Eudora screeched. "Having nails stuck in you sounds more painful than that thing my brother stuck in you."

"No, no, Miz Eudora. They don't hammer nails in you. They beautify your fingernails and toenails."

Miz Eudora glanced down at the red orthopedic shoes on her feet, as if she could see through them to her own toenails.

"Some people say it's a luxury, but I don't like anybody messing with my feet because they're so sensitive," Hattie said. "But I do like the way they feel afterwards. My feet need all the help they can get."

"You know, I might give that a whirl myself," stated Miz Eudora.

I slammed on the brakes in shock. "Excuse me," I apologized, looking over at her. "My foot must have slipped onto the brake pedal.

"Maybe you need a little work done on your feet, too," suggested Miz Eudora.

"MY NAME IS Mrs. Crow," Hattie told the receptionist. "I called earlier about a pedicure and I brought two friends with me who would also like a pedicure."

The receptionist looked down her list of appointments. "And how do you spell that, Mrs. Crow?"

"C-R-O-W, just like the bird," Hattie answered.

"She's a bird, all right," added Miz Eudora with a giggle.

The receptionist informed us that she thought she could work us all into the schedule. Within a few minutes, we were all enjoying the pleasure of each other's company and "a little fancy footwork," as Miz Eudora called it.

"You might need to watch my last toe," warned Hattie. "There's an extra little bump on it."

"You have an extra little bump on your little toe?" asked Miz Eudora. "I wonder what that is. I have one, too."

"Maybe it's a trait of smart people," Miz Eudora's pedicurist suggested with a playful smile.

"Then it must mean your brains are in your foot," Miz Eudora replied, causing everyone in the shop to laugh.

I'm sure they would have laughed even harder if they'd realized she hadn't meant it as a joke.

BY THE TIME we'd all enjoyed pedicures – for which I "spotted them," not wanting Miz Eudora to have a stroke at the cost – and had dinner with Hattie Crow, it seemed we'd known each other for ages. She and Miz Eudora shared a lot in common, yet they were such opposite characters in other ways.

Hattie was very proud of her family and her German heritage, and made their traditional chicken pies for every function she attended, unless it was summer. "Then I make ice cream," she explained.

She had been a third grade teacher – "one of my former students was a state senator," she bragged

– so she still possessed that domineering trait of wanting to be in charge. "'Sargeant in Arms,' my sisters call me," Hattie said with a blushing grin. "They say I can't keep my fingers out of anything."

I saw that firsthand in Ingle's, I had to refrain from saying.

Hattie was to energetic what Miz Eudora was to mountain women – a legacy. Her short, wavy hair had once been dirty blonde, but thanks to "that coloring I put on it," it was now blue. She went to the beauty shop every Saturday morning and "got those long, silver clips put in my hair so that I'd be ready to go shopping after the beauty shop visit and to church on Sunday morning." Church required wearing a hat and gloves and carrying a pocketbook. It usually meant wearing pearls, which she loved and had a lot of.

She'd spent a lot of time as a teenager driving her grandmother around the town of Hickory. The grandmother had not been a very compassionate person, a trait which caused Hattie to be ultra compassionate, not wanting to be like her grandmother. As for the rest of her family, "I have two younger sisters and we were all married in Miller's Lutheran Church. One of them still lives in Hickory, and the other lives in New Bern, North Carolina. We get together each summer at one of the Carolina beaches, so it's a good thing I tan easily," she told us.

Her favorite Sunday supper was a tall glass of cold milk with cornbread crumpled up in it. If it was a special occasion, she had buttermilk and cornbread. She had chickens, so she gathered her own eggs. Hattie loved to cook; she made "chicken salad that's out of this world" and good pecan pies, "but I only eat egg custards, which I never make."

There was no question that she made her own pie crusts when she explained, "I used to make over a hundred pecan pies every Christmas and I gave every one of them away. I always used chopped pecans because if they're whole, you can't cut the pie. With chopped ones, you can slice the pie in eight pieces without hitting a single pecan."

Hattie especially loved cooking for the sick, the lonely and the desperate, but she'd never let anyone know who'd brought the basket of food. "But some people figured it out," she said humbly. "The saying in Hickory was, 'I can sneeze, and Hattie will have a dinner ready for me.'" She then shook her head. "But I don't want anybody doing anything for me," she informed us as she went on to tell us that she still sewed on her grandmother's old sewing machine.

The "human ball of energy" was quick to let

you know that "I do just fine living alone. I can do anything a man can do," she stated, pointing a finger at us. I soon saw that if she really meant business, she'd point both fingers, giving you a "double barrel." Not to mention that you didn't have to wonder about her opinion on something. She was quick to share that with you, usually with a single or double barrel point!

"They say I got that from my grandmother. Everybody called her a broken mold, and said I was just like her. Since I never had any children, they called me 'the last moldy Miller.'"

I couldn't help but laugh at her frankness and her humor. Mabel might have had the bragging rights of being a triplet, but these two women had something worth a lot more. They were soul sisters – identical spirits. I gave a long, examining look at this woman whom we'd run into at the grocery store. After finding such a rare treasure, I wondered whether Miz Eudora would be anxious to go back to Ingle's in search of another.

An "Armistice Baby, born on November 11th," Hattie was, in all, a beautiful person – inside and out. She was quite voluptuous and had the legs of a WWII pin-up, so I suspected she'd gotten many stares as a young woman. I also suspected that she'd had the jealous wrath of Mabel Toast on more than a few occasions.

As we left Hattie's cottage, Miz Eudora and she made a date to churn butter together the next day in Eudora's "brown crock." They even invited me to come learn how, an invitation which I graciously accepted.

"Then we can invite Mabel over and have Toast and butter," Miz Eudora joked.

That was probably the greatest day of my life up to that point. *I didn't know a person* **could** *find so much in Ingle's*, I mused as I pulled out of Miz Eudora's drive later that evening. *No wonder it's the only supermarket in the area. And Miz Eudora was worried about "losing a body" in there. Instead, we found a body!* I thought with a huge smile.

That's how it was that I came to know that there's a lot to be learned from a Crow's feet.

TEN

O Holy Night

I WAS NEARLY finished placing luminaries down my front sidewalk, a tradition Leon and I had shared each Christmas, when I noticed Preacher Jake's car turn onto Downings Creek Road. *Ah, his monthly visit for "dinner" with Miz Eudora*, I figured. *This is the perfect time to take him my little holiday remembrance.* I grabbed one of the loaves of sourdough bread that had come out of the oven a couple of hours before, lovingly wrapped it in red cellophane with a green curly ribbon and headed across the road.

My hand was positioned to knock on the door when I heard Miz Eudora's voice from inside. "Come on in, Sadie. I was hoping you'd join us for dinner. I made a stack pie just for you."

After letting myself in, I saw the two were

engaged in heavy conversation, so I pulled a chair out from the dining table and quietly took a seat.

"What do you mean, you're not coming to the annual Christmas cantata, Miz Eudora?" asked Preacher Jake. "The people in the choir have been working extremely hard and they deserve the congregation's support." His voice was most inviting, but I'd heard her previously vowing not to attend the service. I also knew why she'd made that vow, but I wondered whether she'd share that tidbit with this man whom she so respected.

Are you kidding? my subconscious yelled at me. *Have you forgotten whom you're talking about? Since when has Eudora Rumph bitten her tongue for anyone?* I decided to sit back and enjoy the luncheon entertainment for I knew what was coming.

"They been doing one of them things for near about ten years," she said. "They work for months to sing all them songs nobody's heard of. What's wrong with singing *Silent Night* and *O Little Town of Bethlehem*?"

"The congregation can sing those as hymns." Preacher Jake was trying to be as diplomatic as possible. "The choir likes to sing something special. You know, a little more demanding. They like to feel that they're giving an exceptional offering of their talents to the congregation and to God."

"If they want to give a *real* gift to the congregation and God," insisted Miz Eudora, "they'd ask Mabel to sit in the congregation and listen to it like everyone else."

"Miz Eudora!" her beloved minister exclaimed, a hint of a grin peeking through his best effort at a serious face.

"Well, it's the truth, Preacher, and you know it. She sounds like a wild turkey gobbling right on the front row of the choir. Why, it's a wonder one of the men hasn't shot her during hunting season. Not to mention that she looks even worse with that big old mouth of hers flopping open and shut, open and shut."

With that Miz Eudora did a silent imitation of Mabel. "Maybe that's why the hunters haven't shot her yet. They don't want to drag something that ugly home with them. You can't even pay attention to what that poor choir's singing for watching her make such a spectacle of herself! You know it just as good as I do, and if you say otherwise, you're telling a great old big lie. God knows it's the truth, too, so you'd might as well go ahead and admit it.

"P'SHAA!" she balked as she took a breath and kept going. "That choir started practicing way before she decided she needed to lay claim to John G.'s land. She has no business going in there and messing them up. They'd done fine all this time without her. Why, the only reason she's in the choir anyway is so she can be seen every Sunday and so she can look out and criticize everybody else. Singing in the choir, I reckon!"

She shook her head in disapproval as she placed the plates and silverware from the sideboard on the table. "I'm just glad Mama and Papa can't see her. I believe that would be enough to make Papa go to church at Peckerwood."

"The choir director must think she's pretty good, Miz Eudora," defended Preacher Jake, finally able to break through her ranting and raving. "He's given Mabel a solo."

"What do you mean, Mabel's singing a solo? Land's sakes! The only way she needs to sing is so low that can't nobody hear her."

I followed Miz Eudora into the kitchen and helped her carry out the bowls of food. She never missed a beat as she continued, "Maybe somebody better give that poor choir director a hearing aid for Christmas. And we better pray that Santa comes early so we don't have to hear Mabel bellowing up there in the choir loft like my mule, Clyde."

She chuckled. "I've got a better idea. She can

be in the live nativity. They're always looking for animals for the stable. She can moo like a cow, or baa like a sheep, all she wants in that." Her chuckle turned into an uproar. "Better still, she can be the donkey. That fits her better. Then I wouldn't have to take my jenny. Lucille could use a rest this year."

"Now, now, Miz Eudora," Preacher Jake interjected, fighting to keep a straight face. "God gives us all talents."

"Maybe so," she admitted, "but the best thing Mabel Jarvis can do with hers is to dig a hole and put it in the ground, and then leave it there 'til God comes back to claim it. Lord knows we don't need five or ten more like it."

Preacher Jake, trying as hard as he could to suppress it, doubled over in laughter. The time had come to give up on this battle and enjoy a good meal.

I felt sure he would return to the skirmish after he'd eaten, but as he stood at the door saying his goodbyes, and thanking me for the bread and Miz Eudora for the pecan pie, I decided he had accepted the fact that he'd lost this one. However, his next statement delivered the blow he needed to be victorious.

"I'll be expecting you for the cantata on Sunday evening, Miz Eudora," he said calmly with a broad smile. "I'll even save you a seat on the front row."

"And I'll even drop by and pick you up," I volunteered, making sure this was one showdown I wouldn't miss.

"Maybe I ought to walk in case I need to get home in a hurry," she contradicted.

"Now, Miz Eudora," the preacher started again. But he didn't have to finish the sentence. He could tell by the cheery expression on her face that his favorite parishioner would be there.

"Well, I'll come, Preacher, but only because you are so nice. Consider this the whipped topping on the pecan pie."

I HAD COUNTED down the days until Sunday evening as I wondered whether the evening's sparks would overshadow the July 4th Fireworks Show. Miz Eudora said not a word all the way to the church so I could tell that she was not as enthusiastic about the cantata, *or rather what would happen,* as I was.

As I read the program, I wondered how long it would take her to see that Mabel's name was listed beside the solo for *O Holy Night.*

"Hmmm, this ain't going to be much of a holy

night," blurted Miz Eudora. She sat in the pew Preacher Jake had saved for us, quiet for a few minutes and then she quickly jumped up, her hands holding her stomach. "Sadie, can you run me home for a minute? I forgot something that I really need."

"Is it absolutely necessary, Miz Eudora?" I asked, glancing down at my watch. "It's almost time for the cantata to begin."

"Oh, yes. It's... it's... it's some medicine I need. I'm not sure I can make it through the cantata without it."

"Then we'd better hurry. Surely Preacher Jake will save our places after he's welcomed everyone and said an opening prayer. I don't want to miss a note." *Or a spark!* I wanted to add.

I followed her out the side door of the sanctuary and drove her down the mountain, glad that everyone else in the gap must be at his or her own Christmas cantata, as we buzzed across Highway 64 with no traffic.

"You wait here in the car," she instructed as I came to a quick stop in front of her door. "I'll be right back."

Miz Eudora slipped inside the house, and unbeknownst to me at the time, rushed through the back door and around to the cellar. She grabbed the flashlight she kept hidden inside the cellar door and groped her way to the far corner beside the rutabagas. In no time, she was back in the car and we were headed up the mountain to the church and the cantata.

"Thank you. Thank you kindly, Sadie. I just don't think I could have made it through the night without this medicine."

"Are you sure you're okay, Miz Eudora?" I asked, beginning to feel guilty that I insisted she go through with her promise to Preacher Jack. "I didn't realize you didn't feel well. We really don't have to go to the cantata."

"Don't you worry one iota about me," she said, clamping down on her purse. "I'm going to feel a lot better before the night is over."

"Okay, as long as you say so," I agreed. "If you need to leave, all you have to do is nudge me. I'll take you right back home, and if you need me to stay with you until you feel better, I'll do that, too."

"Thank you, but I'm sure that won't be necessary," she assured me.

I noticed that already her face and her demeanor seemed much improved. *Too bad the medicine for my occasional back spasms doesn't work that fast*, I thought sarcastically.

Miz Eudora excused herself, heading toward the restrooms. Once out of my sight, she made a slight detour through the fellowship hall to where the choir was now congregated as they waited for their cue for the processional. No one paid any attention when she bumped into Mabel, knocking her sister-in-law's bottled lemon water onto the floor.

"Oh, clumsy me!" exclaimed Miz Eudora.

"You klutz!" exclaimed Mabel. "Now look what you've gone and done."

"You stay right here," offered Miz Eudora, "I'll run to the kitchen and fill this bottle back up for you."

While Mabel wiped at the wet spots on her robe, Miz Eudora took off for the kitchen, bottle in hand, and then hastily rushed back. "Here, good as new," she said, handing the bottle to Mabel. "I even found some lemon juice for it in the refrigerator. Now you keep this water handy and remember to take a few sips every little bit to keep your throat in good shape. It will help your solo, you know."

"Whatever happened to Miz Eudora?" asked one of the tenors in the choir. "I've never seen her so interested in Mabel's welfare."

"Yes, isn't it wonderful?" asked one of the sopranos. "It's never too late for an old dog to learn new tricks."

"Old dog is right!" Mabel retorted, taking a

small sip of the water. "Thank God, she found the lemon juice in the refrigerator back there." She took another sip. "This seems to have a little more zest than what I'd brought." She shrugged. "Maybe it's a good thing Eudora bumped into me."

By the time the cantata came to Mabel's solo, she appeared to have loosened up a bit. Her face was all aglow with the Christmas spirit.

Preacher Jake must have noticed, too, for he leaned toward me. "Seems like Miz Eudora's Christmas spirit has rubbed off on her sister-in-law. What a miracle God is working in our little church this year."

Mabel managed to get through the entire solo without a single mistake and even soared over the high notes. I couldn't help but notice that her mouth didn't make its usual overemphasized open and closed motions.

"Look how she's even swaying to the music," whispered a lady behind me.

"I've never seen such a pleasant expression on Mrs. Jarvis' face," added someone else.

"Nor heard so many pleasant notes from her," observed another listener.

Miz Eudora sat quietly listening, her hands folded in her lap. As Mabel belted out the high notes of the final ending of *O Holy Night*, applause erupted in the small sanctuary.

"That was quite lovely," said someone across the aisle. "I never knew Mabel had it in her."

Miz Eudora snickered. "That's right, and you'll never know what Mabel had in her," she muttered under her breath as she patted the small glass bottle inside her purse. "It was a lot more than the right notes!"

When it came time for the choir to recess to the back of the sanctuary, then on to the Fellowship Hall for pick-ups, there was a rhythmic swagger in Mabel's step. One of the men had to hold onto her to make sure she didn't bump into the pews.

"Oh, look!" exclaimed Preacher Jake. "Mabel did such a good job that she must be beside herself. I've never seen her so giddy."

"Giddy-up," replied Miz Eudora. "That's what she better be doing. Much more of that water and she'll be singing from the ceiling fan in the Fellowship Hall. Somebody better get her some coffee."

A puzzled look came over my face as I glared at her. "Miz Eudora, you didn't."

"Didn't what?" she asked innocently.

"You didn't spike the punch, did you?" I asked.

"Land sakes, no! Whatever gave you such an

idea?"

"Just a weird thought, I guess. Mabel doesn't seem quite herself and I thought maybe…,"

"Wasn't Mabel's solo absolutely lovely?" Mrs. Swicegood commented as she passed behind us. "I knew she'd do a fine job once the cantata started. And did you see the expression on her face as she sang? She was certainly full of the Christmas Spirit."

"She was full of the spirit, all right," Miz Eudora replied.

"And how are you feeling now?" Mrs. Swicegood asked Miz Eudora, having overheard the earlier complaint.

"Fine. Just fine," nodded Miz Eudora. "That medicine warded off what was ailing me."

"Medicine?" repeated Preacher Jake as he handed Miz Eudora and me each a cup of punch. "What medicine?"

"Oh, it was only a little something I needed for an earache." Miz Eudora winked at him. "Or should I say, 'a little something' I needed to prevent an earache."

"Miz Eudora, you're terrible," he said.

"P'SHAA! I saved the cantata from being a disaster. I did my part. I'm sure God's angels are all flying around up there in the air and saying what a good job the choir did. Especially Mabel."

I decided to go and offer a compliment to Mabel, who was surrounded by congratulatory admirers. As I glanced around at the group circling her, I noticed I was not the only one who appeared to catch a whiff of something strange. Miz Eudora lowered her head when I looked back in her direction.

On the way home, I informed Miz Eudora that her effort, despite the fact that I thought it was horrible, had added a beautiful touch to the cantata. "But you do know," I added, "that one of these days Mabel will get her harp and she'll be singing in that Angel Band in the sky."

"Honey, it's going to take a lot more than any harp to make that woman sound good," she replied. "All I can say is that we'd better slip a little of Horace's good stuff into her coffin."

"Well, I'll certainly never tell," I said.

"I'll never bake you another stack pie if you do," she warned me.

That's how it was that the congregation of First Church, Smackass, came to have the merriest Christmas they'd ever had, and the most holy night of all.

ELEVEN

The Other White Meat

I'D HEARD TELL of many ways of celebrating New Year's Eve. In fact, my favorite, until my move to Clay County, had been the Walleye that was dropped annually at some of the towns near the Great Lakes. I had no idea what they used to mark the event in Smackass Gap, but I knew it would be the most outlandish thing I'd ever heard of.

I was right!

"Sadie," called Miz Eudora as she reached my front steps. "Sadie, are you home?"

I knew whatever she wanted had to be important for an entrance like that. "What's wrong?" I asked, opening the door for her.

"Nothing's wrong. I wanted to make sure you didn't have plans for New Year's. And I was kind of hoping you might give me a ride to Clay's Corner for the annual Possum Drop."

"Possum Drop?" I repeated slowly.

"Yes. Clay's been doing it for several years now and it's got so big, we had people come from California and England last year. Right here to Clay County they come to see that big old rascal drop at midnight."

"Like the Big Apple?" I asked, trying to picture a lighted up possum in my mind coming from the top of a mountain on a pole as people counted backwards, "Ten, nine, eight...."

"What big apple?" she asked in return.

"The one in...," I stopped myself. If she didn't have a television, I was sure she'd never seen the horde of people in Times Square every December 31st. "It's a tradition they have in New York City each New Year's Eve," I explained, deciding that was all that was necessary on the subject.

"It's a big deal," she said. "The only thing better would be if they dropped Mabel."

How did I not see that coming? I asked myself.

"You're going to have to help me get Mabel there because if I tell her there's a possum involved, I'm sure she won't go."

I wasn't too sure I wanted to go either, but at the same time, I wasn't about to miss this sight. I'd enlist Hattie's help to get Mabel there.

"What exactly do they do at the Possum Drop?" I inquired, not too sure I really wanted to know.

"Well, there's lots of stuff what goes on," she explained. "Clay's got this thing down to a fine art. You know, that man's so creative. Sometimes I hate I don't live over about Brasstown because he's always got something fun and exciting going on. I've heard they play BINGO near there every little bit and I sure would like to go sometime if it's not too much trouble."

I smiled at her innocence, which never ceased to amaze me and warm my heart. "I'm sure we can work that out."

"Maybe we can go this week," she suggested. "I heard one of the women in my Sunday School class say that they're doing Grocery BINGO this week. I don't know if that means you bring groceries, or you win groceries, but whatever it is, it sounds fun. I might need you to take me to Ingle's on the way."

"Only if you promise to keep your fingers out of the pimento cheese," I warned.

"I promise," she said with a big grin. "Maybe I'll try the chicken salad instead."

I winced as Miz Eudora paused for a moment.

"Oh, that won't do," she decided. "That's Hattie's specialty. I'll have to figure out something else."

"Why don't you take a jar of your home-canned hominy?" I was quick to suggest. "That always seems to be a favorite around here."

I was grateful that my idea seemed to satisfy her. "So, back to the Possum Drop," I hastily continued, more as an effort to keep her mind off of going to Ingle's.

"Well, it gets started about ten o'clock and there's all kinds of things what goes on until midnight," Miz Eudora began. "It starts off with a blessing. There's a group of men, called the Brasstown Brigade, that gather from here, Murphy and Andrews and bring their muzzle-loaders and do a chant asking for good fortune over the possum and for everyone's New Year. Then they shoot off the guns. I understand it's some sort of German tradition. Supposedly, they do it in some other places where they begin at midnight and go from door to door chanting and blessing and having cups of cheer. I've heard tell that it'll go on until way over into New Year's Day. I hope those cups of cheer they have weren't like Horace's. They might haul off and bless or shoot the wrong thing!"

She snickered briefly. "Now there's an idea.

Maybe we can sneak them a cup of Horace's cheer and they can relieve us of Mabel."

I gave her a scrutinizing shake of the head, trying to pretend that wasn't my same thought.

"Then there's the Miss Possum Contest where some of the men dress up as women to see who wins the crown for the year." She leaned toward me and I knew what was next. "They're not funny or nothing. It's all done in good fun."

I nodded, letting her know that I understood, as she sat aright again.

"It's a big job," she said emphatically, "just like with Miss America, because the winner has to show up at all the organized events during the year, like the Midnight Walks up Dog Branch.

"After that, the little Brasstown Baptist choir comes and sings old time gospel songs and then there's a tribute to our servicemen. By the time they do all that, it's time to lower the possum and shoot the fireworks. It really just depends as to what time that actually happens because there's a lot of things to happen and go wrong during those two hours."

During all her raving about the event, I couldn't help but wonder about the poor animal that was dropped. I had all kinds of visions, most of them unpleasant, about what happened on the stroke of midnight.

"Is it a real possum, and what do they do with the possum after he drops?" I finally ventured.

"Land sakes!" she bellowed. "What kind of animals do you think we are?"

"I think Clay borrowed somebody's pet possum for a couple of years. We used to have this big deal where the men would get together and go out in search of just the right possum. That was just a made up tale to add fun to the event, but the men did get together for a day of good times. But then, them thar people what gets all out of whack about animals got wind of it and had such a fit that Clay had to find a roadkill possum to use and fluff it all up with a hairdryer to make it look alive."

"P'SHAA!" she exclaimed with disdain. "It was probably one of the roadkill possums that one of them animal people run over on their way up the mountain, while they was busy making sure we wasn't mistreating the possum. They've done a lot more harm with all the possums they've run over and left beside the road than we've ever thought about doing. Clay puts the possum in this real nice plexiglass cage and it goes down real slow. When it reaches the ground, the possum runs on off about his business. You can't get any nicer to an animal than that. Why, that possum's got the best view in the crowd. Plus he don't have to stand suffocating in a big bunch of people who've come from everywhere to watch him in the 'O'possum Taj Mahal' that Clay made for him.

"I didn't mean any harm," I quickly added, before she got upset, "I just wasn't sure."

"Now Clay does have some big artificial critter rigged up at the store for tourists who come by the rest of the year," she explained. "But about tonight, don't tell Mabel anything about it. I want to see the expression on her face when that thing starts down the pole, peering out at the ground in his aerial search for all the beetles, cockroaches and slugs he's going after when he gets down."

Her face took on that winsome appearance. "You know, Clay is such a fine feller. He has a big possum costume that he takes around to the schools to talk to the students about staying off drugs. I've heard he even has coloring books that he gives out to them, too. He calls the possum Opie. Ain't that the finest name you ever did hear for a possum?"

I'd never really considered a name, good or bad, for a possum, but I thought that might make for an interesting conversation with Hattie and Mabel on the way home from Clay's Corner after the big night.

"Some people wouldn't understand our culture and our tradition here," Miz Eudora said candidly. "But it's all about having a good time safely and involving our kids. Clay's made a good thing out of Brasstown being the O'Possum Capital of the World. He's even got some bumper stickers down there that say, 'Possum, the other white meat.' Horace had one on his pick-up truck.

"I reckon that's what all the men that meet down there every morning do. They sit around that stove and play checkers and make up sayings about Clay's pet possum, Opie. Which is all right," she concluded. "It keeps them out of trouble. They can't be making moonshine and carousing around if they're thinking up stuff about the possum."

Now that's certainly an interesting way to think of the possum, I mused.

"I have an idea," I said. "Why don't we not even tell Hattie and Mabel where we're going and I'll simply surprise them? Brasstown is too far for them to walk home, so once we get there, they'll have to stay until it's all over."

"Sadie, you're so smart," she said with a big smile. "Sometimes I forget you ain't a regular around here," which was her way of saying I wasn't a native of Smackass Gap. It was also her way of saying I was as "all right" as possum and hog jowls.

That's how it was that I came to learn that possum is the other white meat.

TWELVE

A Red Hat Valentine

QUEEN ANGELBREEZE HAMMERED the red wooden gavel on the table. "I now call this meeting of the Hot G.R.I.T.S. 'n' Red Hats to order."

"I warned you," Mabel said to Eudora, "I'm not eating any grits. If I didn't eat them at Myers Park, I'm not eating them anywhere."

"Oh, hush up, Mabel," Miz Eudora scorned quietly, "that's just their name. That's not what they're serving. Besides, it stands for 'Girls Raised in the South,'" she beamed, sharing the knowledge she'd learned on their bus trip together.

Miz Eudora playing the quiet sidekick was a switch, given she could usually rile any situation at a moment's notice. As I watched the two, who appeared to be rapidly brewing into a female Laurel and Hardy routine, I prayed we wouldn't be banned before we were even welcomed into the group.

"We have four new members tonight, meaning that we have reached our limit of twenty as the number of members we can have in our chapter," Queen Angelbreeze proudly announced. "Three of them we met on our recent outing through Clay County, North Carolina, on our way to Atlanta. You'll all remember Miz Eudora Rumph, of course," Her words were interrupted by welcoming giggles and nods of heads as all the ladies waved at Miz Eudora. "And her sister-in-law, Mabel Jarvis."

"Don't be spreading that word," piped up Miz Eudora. "There might be some folk here what don't know that. We wouldn't want them to get a bad impression of me." Her response caused more energetic giggles. It also caused a great big huff by Mabel, whose face was taking on the color of her red hat.

"Our other two new members are Sadie Calloway, who you also met at our outing when she came to get Miz Eudora down in Georgia, and their friend, Hattie Crow, who heard about all the fun we had on that trip and has asked to join us, hoping for a chance at a trip with Miz Eudora.

"We also have our friend, Barbara, visiting with us from the Smokin' Babes Chapter. She heard that Miz Eudora was going to be here this evening and decided she didn't want to miss anything should there be any more excitement."

You have Eudora Rumph and Mabel Jarvis in the same room and you wonder if there's going to be any excitement? I wondered. *Maybe I should tell them Mabel's maiden name. That ought to light a spark that will keep them going for a while.* However, deciding those two didn't need an instigator, I sat back to let them create their own excitement, knowing it wouldn't be a long wait.

Queen Angelbreeze completed her introductions and passed out the New Member information sheets. "You'll each be asked to come up with a royal name, which should have something to do with you. You can be a lady or a princess or a jester, whatever you wish, but you can't be the queen. I'm the queen of this chapter.

"For instance, my name is Queen Angelbreeze because I like angels and I love wind chimes. You choose a name that reflects something about you."

"I hope yours is something we can say out loud," Miz Eudora said, snickering and punching Mabel with her elbow. Her comment sent trickles of muffled laughter around the room.

Here we go, I said to myself, preparing for the soon-to-be roller coaster ride. *It won't be long now.*

"And I suppose you have something in mind for yours?" Mabel asked.

"I sure do! I'm going to be Lady Eudora Rumphfelter. I always did wonder what it felt like to be one of them proper ladies.

"You're a lady, alright," retorted Mabel. "A lady-in-waiting and you're going to be waiting a very long time!"

The trickles of laughter were no longer muffled.

"What made you decide to add the 'felter' to the end of your name, Miz Eudora?" Peggy ventured.

Her question caused me to cower, for I sensed we were already on the start of an adventure. I still feared that our first meeting might also be our last. But then I looked at Miz Eudora in that purple fopher coat and that red hat and realized we were on an adventure, all right. The very kind of adventure that rescued all these women from the "old hat" comfort of their own home and the mundane, and sometimes critical, issues of life that had happened upon them when they turned the corner at the age of fifty. With that realization, I sat back in the plush Queen Anne armchair in the living room of the hostess and buckled my proverbial seatbelt as I awaited Miz Eudora's response.

"Because there's a family named Clodfelter

back up on Chunky Gal Mountain," she explained, "and that's about the most royal name I ever heard."

"We welcome Lady Eudora Rumphfelter into the Hot G.R.I.T.S. 'n' Red Hats," Queen Angelbreeze declared. "Have you thought of a name yet, Mabel?"

"I'm thinking about Countess Camellia Laurel. I had several camellia bushes in my yard in Charlotte, and I've always liked the Mountain Laurel of the mountains." She eyed Miz Eudora. "It's about the only thing good that came out of the mountains besides my dearly departed John G." Mabel looked back at the group.

"Countess Laurel...now that's a good one for you," Miz Eudora said with a nod. "Papa always did say you wasn't count for much besides sitting on your laurels."

"Well, I never!"

"No, you sure didn't ever hit a lick at nothing. That's exactly why Papa said that."

The other women lowered their heads to avoid fits of laughter. I adjusted my proverbial seat belt a little bit tighter as I spotted a full-fledged row between the two "on the horizon."

Mabel took off her jacket and began to fan with her New Member information sheet. "These blamed old hot flashes. They only seem to hit at the most inopportune times."

Nods of heads showed understanding, although I highly suspected the sudden heat wave came from Miz Eudora's comment rather than a rise in temperature, especially since it was quite cool for a Southern night.

"Here, I'll crack the door a bit," offered Debbie, the hostess of the meeting, whose home in Highlands was serving as the boxing ring for the evening.

"Why don't you just take off your shirt, Mabel?" invited Vickie. "We're all women here."

"Lord, have mercy!" shot Miz Eudora, spewing iced tea across the room and causing several women to reach for napkins. "There are just *some things* in life that a body don't need to see."

Mabel huffed again and fanned harder.

"You're welcome to stand over here in front of the door for a few minutes," offered Debbie. "I'm sure some of the other ladies are probably hot, too."

"You got that right!" called Hattie. "Hot flashes, cold cream, hot flashes, cold cream. Seems all I do anymore is have hot flashes and pile on the cold cream."

"You don't use cold cream to make you cooler," replied Marlene.

"I know that. I use it on my face to keep me from looking older." Hattie combed her short hair with her fingers. "I'm a princess, you know. Princess Prudence," she said, giving the royal name she'd chosen, "and princesses can't look like old hags."

"Princess Prudence," Queen Angelbreeze announced, taking control of the meeting while she had the chance. "Our next meeting will be February 13th," she continued. "We'll meet at the Jarrett House in Dillsboro for our Valentine's get-together."

"The Jarrett House," repeated several of the women.

"I love their little biscuits and the honey," said Mary Beth.

"My favorite is the country ham and red eye gravy," added Vickie. "My parents used to go to the Jarrett House every time they'd go through the western part of North Carolina and they say the food still tastes the same."

"Yes, you definitely need to come hungry," Queen Angelbreeze informed them.

"And save room for the vinegar pie," suggested Marlene. "It's the best I've ever had."

"Vinegar pie?" asked Mabel. "Ugh!"

"The way your face looks, Mabel, you'd think you eat vinegar pie every morning for breakfast," Miz Eudora replied.

Queen Angelbreeze was quick to respond with, "Everyone needs to bring a Valentine box for herself and a little card for everyone else. Be sure to write a special message for each member on the back of the cards."

"Oh, what fun! I haven't done that since grade school," Mary Beth remarked.

Several of the women made comments about the activity as it brought back a flood of childhood memories for them.

"What's a Valentine box?" asked Miz Eudora.

"You know, one of those boxes like you used to make at school to collect your Valentine cards," explained Rita.

"Honey, we was so poor that didn't nobody have a box. If we was lucky, one person in the family got a new pair of shoes at Christmas, whichever one's turn it was for that year, and the box, if there was one, had been put to good use by my mama. If us young'uns had paper, we'd make our own Valentines, and we'd carry them home in the sack we'd carried our lunch to school in."

Miz Eudora's statement left a somber feeling among the group as they looked around at each other, their eyes suddenly sharing a desire to do something more.

"You just gave me an idea, Miz Eudora,"

stated Peggy. "Why don't we each put the money we'd spend for our monthly raffle tickets in a jar at that meeting and use the money to do something special for a child?" She hung her head. "Sadly, there's poverty-stricken children in most every community anymore."

"That gives me another idea," Barbara piped up. "A restaurant at home has a mascot, Rudy the Red Pig. He's collecting books for children in the Gulf who still have no books. Why don't we each take a children's book to donate?"

"I've got a better idea!" suggested Rita. "I read last week in the paper where Rudy is taking some people with him in his Bookmobile to the Gulf to read the books to all those boys and girls who still can't go to school. Why don't we make that one of our projects? We could go down there with Rudy."

"We'd never all fit in that poor little pig's Bookmobile. There wouldn't be any room for the books," said Marlene.

"Well then, we'll all pile into vans," Rita responded. "I'll drive mine."

"What's wrong with the bus you had when you picked me up?" asked Miz Eudora. "That was the finest ride I ever had in my life. Why, it even had indoor plumbing on it."

Murmurs and nods sprung up from around the room.

"She's right," said Vickie. "That trip was a blast. Besides, that's when we met Miz Eudora, Sadie and Mabel. Just think, we might pick up some other prospective Red Hatter members on the way to the Gulf."

The murmurs got louder and the nods more energized.

"What if we invite Red Hatters from other chapters to go with us so we could fill up the bus?" suggested Peggy.

"Now's that's what I'd call a trip!" added Mary Beth. "A *real* Red Hat trip!"

"How sweet!" voiced Hattie. "We Red Hatters are going to help our little red friend."

"Except that he's not so little," explained Barbara. "He's over six feet tall."

"That's it," announced Queen Angelbreeze. "We'll find out when Rudy is making his next trip to the Gulf and we'll all go with him. I'll start calling for bus rental rates tomorrow."

A huge cheer broke out in the room as I sat mesmerized at the spontaneity of this group of women. I wondered if all their meetings were this convivial. As I peered at each one, I wondered about their marital status, and whether they'd been this eager to drop everything and go their entire lives. *But then,* I reasoned, *I guess this is one self-acclaimed award for living this long, surviving kids, jobs, spouses...*

Then it hit me. *Surviving...period!* Watching them in their outrageous attire and red hats, they truly did hold a key for living that a lot of women were missing.

"Well, I'm going to tell you right now," warned Mabel, "I'm not telling my friends that I'm traveling all the way to the Gulf with a red pig. As far as I'm concerned, he's nothing more than a scarlet swine, I don't care how sweet he is."

"Land sakes, Mabel! What in tarnation are you carrying on for? All your friends *are* swine. Leastways, them what's not...well, I won't say that animal in front of these nice ladies, but let's put it this way. You got nothing to worry about." With that, she whipped around to the rest of the group and without missing a beat, asked, "Do I have to sit beside Mabel all the way down there?"

Her question caused the loud murmurs to turn to raucous laughter.

"I think Miz Eudora ought to get to sit on the front seat behind the driver," declared Barbara. "After all, this whole idea came about because of her."

"Yes, and all the rest of us can take turns sitting in the other front seat," added Mary Beth.

"Oh, this is going to be so much fun. I can't wait," said Vickie.

"Well, before I forget, I'd better write down the date of our Valentine meeting," replied Rita. "I can't seem to remember anything anymore."

"I'll bet you don't forget our trip we're going to take with Rudy and Miz Eudora," stated Marlene.

"No, I surely won't forget that." Rita paused. "At least, I hope not. I bought myself some of that Gingko Biloba at the grocery store to help me remember, but I forgot where I put it."

The women laughed, but although it was a joke, I could see from their faces that Rita wasn't the only Red Hatter suffering from that problem.

"Hey," Miz Eudora spoke up, "if that stuff makes you forget, somebody buy some for Mabel. I'll be glad to pay for it. Then maybe she'll miss the bus." She peered at the dumbfounded expression on her sister-in-law's face. "Oh, never mind. She's already missed the bus. Buying that…whatever you called it would just be a waste of good money!"

Mabel hissed and puffed up. I couldn't help but think she both looked and sounded like an old pressure cooker about to blow its top. I'm glad Miz Eudora didn't see it that way, for one more comment from her and I believe the top would have blown.

Luckily Queen Angelbreeze changed the subject. "It's time for our raffle. Who brought the gift for tonight?" she asked, sounding as royal as a queen demanding to know who'd brought a sacrifice for the throne.

Mabel seemed a logical choice for a sacrifice, as it seemed she was sacrificed every time Miz Eudora opened her mouth. Suddenly I envisioned her as a pig, complete with an apple in her mouth, lying sprawled atop a silver tray on a royal banquet table. I contemplated suggesting they let her sit with Rudy the Scarlet Swine on the way to the Gulf, but that would have been "icing on the cake" rather than "glaze over the ham."

"PEGGY!" everyone answered in unison, drawing my attention away from Mabel and the pig and back to raffle tickets.

Peggy picked up a rather large gift bag and moved to stand beside the queen.

"Okay, Peggy, you get to decide on the amount for the tickets," instructed Queen Angelbreeze. "Did someone bring the tickets?" she asked, glancing around the room.

"I did," Marlene quickly answered, whipping a roll of tickets out of her tote bag.

"Oh, look!" exclaimed Vickie. "She even got

the double roll."

"Well, it wouldn't have done much good otherwise," Marlene shot back. "How would we have known who had the winning number?"

"The tickets are going to be fifty cents each," announced Peggy.

Women started digging in their purses for change and dollar bills. I noticed that Rita even had a roll of quarters tucked inside her jacket pocket, reading for the big drawing. They each called out the number of tickets they wanted as Peggy and Marlene moved about the room taking up money and distributing tickets.

"Make mine the winner," instructed Mary Beth.

"Nope, I'm going to be the winner this time," Vickie challenged.

"Don't you want any tickets, Miz Eudora?" asked Peggy, seeing she had no money in her hand.

"No, ma'am, I'll pass," Miz Eudora answered solemnly. "I don't rightly believe in gambling."

"You don't do nothing 'rightly,' Eudora," said Mabel, who had her money ready. "Just play along."

"It isn't gambling, Miz Eudora," explained Queen Angelbreeze. "This is a fun way of getting extra money for our chapter. We use it for little things throughout the year."

"Yes, like buying birthday cards and such," added Mary Beth.

"And projects like helping Rudy," continued Vickie.

"In that case," Miz Eudora agreed, "I'll take one ticket. Isn't that all it takes to win?"

"Yes, that's right, as long as yours gets chosen for the winning number."

"I'll stick to one. I won Horace at a church box lunch social, and look what that got me. I don't want to take too much of a chance."

"Hmmph," snorted Mabel, handing Peggy three one-dollar bills.

"Has everyone gotten all the tickets they want?" questioned Queen Angelbreeze. Seeing that each of the women had tickets in her hands, she continued. "Okay, Peggy, you choose someone to do the honors of drawing the winning ticket."

"Countess Camellia Laurel, since you're new to our chapter, why don't you do the honors?" asked Peggy, giving a curtsy to one of their newest members of Red Hat royalty.

"I'd be delighted," Mabel answered, giggling at Peggy's antics.

"But don't peek," warned Mary Beth, "in case you draw one of your own numbers. Then you'll still get to keep the prize."

Mabel reached in the box containing the ticket stubs, drew out one and looked at it. With a playful twinkle in her eye, she glanced around the room and gave a loud, "AH-OOO-OOO!" startling everyone in the room.

"Cut the crap, Mabel, and give Peggy the ticket," ordered Miz Eudora. She looked around at the other women, who were as horrified by her comment as they were Mabel's screech. "She does that every time she opens a present. First time she and John G. came to Smackass Gap for Christmas, Papa thought someone had let the old barn owl in the house."

Mabel pursed her lips and handed the ticket to Peggy.

"The winning number is 45873," Peggy announced.

All of the women looked closely at their tickets.

"Missed again," said Rita.

One after another, comments of playful disappointment echoed.

"Check your numbers," suggested Peggy. "It has to belong to someone. 45873," she called again.

"Hey, that's my number," crowed Miz Eudora. "Thank you, Mabel." She acknowledged her sister-in-law with an appreciative grin.

Peggy held out a decorative red-and-purple striped gift bag. "Congratulations, Lady Eudora Rumphfelter."

"Show us what you got," urged Vickie.

Miz Eudora pulled out the red tissue paper with one hand and a shiny purple, handled cosmetic bag with the other. "Ain't that pretty? I'll be the talk of the church when I show up with this on Sunday morning." She hung it on her forearm like a purse. "I'll bet Preacher Jake even makes a comment about it when I'm going out the door after the service."

"For goodness sakes, Eudora," scoffed Mabel, "it isn't a purse. It's to put your make-up and such in." She turned to the rest of the group. "Eudora's never seen a bit of make-up her entire life," she said in a disdaining tone.

"No wonder her face still looks like a peach," observed Mary Beth. "Well, Lady Eudora, you can use it on our trip with Rudy. I'm sure you can find something to put in it."

"Yes," Miz Eudora responded, "it's too bad I can't roll Mabel up and put her in it. Then we could stick her underneath the bus where all you ladies had your shopping bags before."

"Keep digging, Lady Eudora. There's more," said Barbara.

All eyes were on Miz Eudora as she retrieved a bar of soap and a candle, both lavender-scented, from the bag.

"How dandy!" she exclaimed. "Now I won't have to be in such a rush to make the next batch of lye soap. I was near 'bout out. And what a nice candle. Maybe I can light a fire under one of them varmint jackets of Mabel's with it. That would save that poor old hound dog of the neighbor's a lot of howling. He's been trying to tree one of them things ever since she showed up in Smackass Gap."

The last item was a large glass decanter with purple crystals. Miz Eudora looked puzzled as she turned the decanter around in her hands so that she could read the bottle. "What in tarnation?"

"Haven't you ever seen bath salts before?" asked Marlene.

"Bath salts? Is that what this is? Why, sure, I've seen bath salts," answered Miz Eudora with a nod. "It's just that they come in a cardboard carton at home." She leaned forward and whispered, with a large shy smile, "I've even had a take a dose or two every once in a while."

"Eudora, really!" huffed Mabel.

"Really, I did," defended Miz Eudora. "We used them for other things, too," she shared with the Red Hatters, "like when Horace had to soak his feet, or needed to draw swelling or pus out of a sore."

"These are different, Miz Eudora," explained Mary Beth. "They're not that kind of salts."

"These salts are to put in the bathtub," Barbara continued. "You use them when you take a bath and they'll make you feel and smell really nice."

"Yes, you can really feel like a lady when you use those," added Rita.

"It's going to take more than any bath salts to make her a lady," Mabel grunted. "Hmmph! She doesn't even have a bathtub in her house. She's still using that big washtub."

"That doesn't matter," Hattie replied, trying to play referee. "They'll still make her look and feel nice."

"Nice, I reckon!" exclaimed Miz Eudora, ignoring her sister-in-law, as usual. "Thank you, ladies, for telling me all about the purple bath salts. And thank you, Peggy, for all the nice presents. And to think I won with only one ticket. I'm sure glad this present was better than winning Horace."

"I think it's time to adjourn and go home," said Queen Angelbreeze. "Don't forget, our next meeting will be at the Jarrett House on February 13th. I'll make our reservation tomorrow. How many of you want to go?" Queen Angelbreeze counted hands. "Great, that's all of us. We'll find out then about the Gulf trip and begin making our plans."

"Be sure to invite the Red Hat Nanny. This sounds right down her alley," Marlene added.

"Do you think Rudy will be there?" asked Miz Eudora. "We've raised plenty of hogs in my time, but I never seen a red one before."

"I'll call and see if maybe he can make a special appearance," Barbara offered.

"While you're calling, why don't you see if the Chippendales are available?" snickered Rita.

"Rita! Really…," scorned Marlene.

"I was just kidding," Rita replied, shaking her head in disbelief that anyone would have taken her suggestion to heart.

"Oh, c'mon, you two," said Peggy. "We all know it wouldn't have upset you one bit if those guys showed up at our Valentine's event."

"Or any other event for that matter," added Debbie, getting in on the joke.

"Yeah, it would be fun to see Peggy running down to the closest convenient store to change all those 20-spots she carries into one-dollar bills!" exclaimed Mary Beth, causing laughter to erupt throughout the room.

"That's enough, girls! Do I have to put you in opposite corners?" Queen Angelbreeze interrupted.

She cleared her throat, signaling that she was ready for the conversation to return to a serious note.

Personally, I liked the direction it was going. Every woman present was letting loose and laughing, no harm intended and none taken, all while enjoying the gift of the best medicine. Apparently, I wasn't the only one who felt that way, for the only response she got was that Mabel, who had begun fanning harder, jumped up and rushed to the door which she began swinging back and forth to sweep the cool air from outside into the room.

"That's right," signaled Debbie, pointing to Mabel. "We'd be having more than hot flashes if those guys showed up."

"Well, you know good and well that they'd surely be 'showing up' if they saw all of us 'Smokin' Babes,'" Barbara continued, causing the laughter that had died down a bit to diminish into embarrassed snickers.

"That's right," agreed Peggy. "It would be like when we were teenagers. Remember when some cute guy would walk by and someone would yell out, 'Guy on the beach,' That was our signal to suck it in and look our best."

"I saw the Chippendales one time," said Miz Eudora nonchalantly, rubbing her hand across her red leather purse and not even looking up.

All laughter halted as heads turned toward her in shock. I even heard a couple of the women gasp in chorus with Mabel. The others gazed at her, some with a look of jealousy, some with a look of admiration.

"They were pretty cute fellers," she began. "Really furry. I think they're furrier than the ones we got in Smackass Gap."

"I think we're getting too much information," Marlene whispered to Hattie, who nodded in agreement.

"The way Mabel likes wearing things around her neck," Miz Eudora went on, "she ought to give those boys a whirl. I'll bet they'd get her plenty of stares going down the street."

Several pairs of eyes darted toward Mabel's fox stole while the rest of the eyes hit the floor.

"Hey, that might be a good idea," Barbara said, picking up on the image Miz Eudora was creating. "I'll bet we could make lots of money for the Smokin' Babes if we sold those stoles at our next event."

"Or had our hat contest to include making a stole of some kind to match," suggested Vickie.

"Hush up!" ordered Peggy. "I want to hear."

"Ahem!" shouted Queen Angelbreeze, determined to regain control of the meeting.

Obviously she wasn't as determined as the women who were now caught up in the image of the Chippendales. "So tell us, Miz Eudora," asked Marlene, "where exactly did you see the Chippendales?"

"It was one afternoon at the home of one of our quilters from the church," Miz Eudora began.

You could have heard a pin drop as suddenly the room filled with thoughts of eighty and ninety-year-old women, who could have been the epitome of the grandmothers of every woman at this meeting, piled onto sofas and chairs with their eyes gawking.

"She had a television set in her house," continued Miz Eudora, "and when her little great-grandson came in from playschool, he brought some movie with him. It was so entertaining that we all sat down and watched it with him." She gave a quiet chuckle. "We all had the best time watching them two cute little fellers getting themselves into so much trouble. Reminded me of lots of young'uns around Smackass Gap."

Miz Eudora stopped and stared at all the eyes glued on her. "You know, if them little chipmunks on Chunky Gal Mountain were nearly that cute, I wouldn't be setting traps for them all the time and I sure wouldn't mind them running all through my garden."

I noted that Queen Angelbreeze now had no trouble getting the attention of the group. They were all speechless that they had been so duped by this laidback, simple mountain woman.

"Well," Queen Angelbreeze stated, in her usual calm tone, "I *do* have some very special entertainment lined up for that evening. We'll have a good time."

"We *always* have a good time," declared Debbie.

Although there was no doubt that her statement was true, I wagered they wouldn't get any better entertainment than they'd had this evening. *Especially for the price!* I reasoned. The looks on the various faces said they'd all had a marvelous time.

"I think we've all witnessed that fact this evening," agreed Marlene with a coy smile.

*I was right. They **did** have a marvelous time!* I told myself, thinking it was too bad my odds weren't that good at Harrah's.

"Miz Eudora, Mabel, Hattie and Sadie, we're thrilled to have all of you as new members," concluded Queen Angelbreeze, "and we're certainly glad you joined us this evening. We'll look forward to seeing you at the Jarrett House."

"Somebody really ought to check to see if

that pig can't go with us on the bus trip," suggested Miz Eudora. "He and Countess Camellia Laurel can sit on their laurels together." She snickered. "I'll even bring a shot of Horace's finest for the countess and they can take turns snorting on the back seat!"

Fearing another outbreak, Queen Angelbreeze quickly announced, "Meeting adjourned!"

That's how it was that I came to understand the meaning of a Red Letter Day, or rather, "a Red Hatter Day!"

THIRTEEN

Pulling Weeds

"GOOD MORNING, LADIES!" greeted the slim-and-trim, bleached blonde as she tried to speak over the din of thirty women. Looking to be in her late twenties, she was dressed in a pink-and-gray striped acrylic sports top and solid pink shorts that might as well have been meshed to her skin. "Welcome to Fitness After Fifty. I'm Trish and I'm going to be your instructor."

"If it's Fitness After Fifty, how come she looks twenty-five?" roared Miz Eudora, her voice as loud as Trish's had been with a microphone. "I think we got cheated. It should have only cost half price if she's only half the age."

The comment was so loud that Trish must have surely heard it, for it was obvious that everyone else in the room did, but she swiftly moved on through her introduction. "Before we start, ladies," she instructed, "be sure to tuck in your buttocks."

"Tuck in our buttocks?" repeated Miz Eudora questioningly. "Are you hanging out back there, Mabel?" she asked with a rather loud guffaw, not bothering to glance at her sister-in-law on the row behind her. "I told you that get-up was way too tight. There's no way it's going to stretch enough to cover up all of you. It must not have a seam or it would have already ripped wide open."

By now, every eye in the room was on Miz Eudora as she turned around to give a snicker in Mabel's direction. "While you're at it, you'd better tuck in a few other places, too."

"Hush up, Eudora, and listen to the teacher," Mabel retaliated. "We paid a lot of money for this," she stated as she adjusted her purple spandex leggings.

"We, nothing," corrected Miz Eudora. "You paid a lot of money for Hattie, Sadie and me to join you because you were too embarrassed to come by yourself. If it hadn't been for the chance to stop by The Fam for chicken livers afterwards, I wouldn't be here, free or not. You can thank Tommy Hooper for this one."

Trish loaded an upbeat musical CD into the stereo system and took her place on the facility's small stage, which was the perfect height for everyone in the class to see her demonstrate the exercise movements. I recognized the music to **Light My Fire**. As I took a quick scan of the others assembled in the room, I couldn't help but wonder if I might be the only one to recognize it. "To start this morning," she yelled over the music, "we're going to do an exercise called, 'Pulling Weeds.'"

"Pulling weeds?" mimicked Miz Eudora. "What's so special about this? Land sakes, Mabel! I could have stayed home and done this and it wouldn't have cost you a dime. I had plenty of weeds you could have pulled. Whose hair-brained idea was this?" She gave another laugh. "It certainly couldn't have been yours, because you don't have a brain, bald *or* with hair!"

I squelched the urge to laugh by bending my knees and stretching my arms forward to pull the imaginary weeds. Hattie and Miz Eudora also began to do the exercise in step with the aerobics instructor, while Mabel stood behind us, grunting with each movement. Her spandex was pulled so tightly in places that, like Miz Eudora, I was surprised it didn't rip with each movement. On the other hand, I noticed that neither Hattie nor Miz Eudora – both dressed in their red hats and purple attire, with the exception of each sporting a new pair of red Converse high-tops – had any difficulty with mobility.

"Are you burning yet, ladies?" Trish called out between counts.

Aha! I concluded. ***No wonder she's playing 'Light My Fire.'***

"Burning?" This time, Miz Eudora's question sounded slightly indignant. "Nobody said nothing about them lighting a fire under us. What does she plan to do? Cook the ham hocks we're supposedly going to lose?" Miz Eudora stopped pulling weeds and stood straight. "Much more of these shenanigans and I'm out of here."

I didn't bother to tell her the name of the music playing for fear that, excuse the pun, it would "fan the flame" that was already rising within her.

"Oh, Eudora, relax!" ordered Mabel. "She means, 'Are your muscles aching yet?'"

"Muscles aching yet? P'SHAA! I should have known that young pipsqueak doesn't know anything about pulling weeds! Why, we just got started. We haven't even done three decent sized tomato plants yet. Surely she's going to do an entire row."

"Breath, ladies. That's the important part," Trish instructed as she walked among the class participants.

"How long did it take her to figure that out?

Breathing, I reckon! We sure can't be pulling no weeds if we ain't breathing," Miz Eudora observed, her words directed at no one in particular.

I could already tell that she was going to be "the last man" – excuse me – "the last lady standing," by the time of the session's end. *Including the prissy instructor*, I wagered.

"Do you feel that tightening in your triceps?" Trish asked.

"I was burning *everywhere*, not just in my triceps," commented one woman in the front row.

She must have been the teacher's pet in grade school, I surmised from the sing-song quality of her voice as she made the statement, not to mention the fact that she was on the front row right in front of the stage. *Even at this age, I guess there's still one in every crowd.*

"Now where are those triceps?" inquired Mabel, huffing from the slightly strenuous exercises, as she felt around on her arms.

"They're right below the biceps," piped up Hattie, who was still keeping up with Trish.

"Do the triceps come with French fries?" asked Miz Eudora.

"Oh, Miz Eudora, you crack me up," Trish said with a giggle, no longer able to ignore the back-and-forth bantering between the two women on the second and third rows.

"From the looks of you," observed Miz Eudora, "I'd say you was already cracked up. Looks like there ain't but half of you here now. We don't want you to be quartered."

"Eudora, please," insisted Mabel, her cheeks matching the red of her oversized tunic. "Don't be insulting the instructor."

"Who's insulting?" Miz Eudora defended. "If the purpose of this Fitness After Fifty place is to lose a bunch of weight, she must have been a good student because there ain't much there. Besides," she continued, quickly turning her comment back to the aerobics teacher, "if I was going to crack somebody up, it would be Mabel anyway, so you've got nothing to worry about." She then turned to me, a smirk covering her entire face. "Mabel's got enough crack for everybody in here."

I coughed hard to cover the outburst of laughter, as did several other participants.

"Let's try this now, ladies." Trish promptly set to bending straight over, placing her hands on the floor so that she was on her "all fours." "We're going to walk our hands straight out in front of us and then back, keeping our feet in place at first. Once we have that, we'll move our hands and then our feet. Kind of like we're on an imaginary ladder, but the ladder is on the floor."

"What do we want to do that for?" Miz Eudora asked, watching Trish demonstrate the exercise. "We've still got the peppers and peas to weed." She watched the demonstration for a few seconds before turning to Hattie, who seemed to be giving Trish a run for her money. "I never seen nobody walk on their hands like that."

"Uh!" Mabel groaned at Miz Eudora's crassness.

"I've seen the crabs at the beach walk like that," Hattie said. "People sometimes do this same exercise, except with their hands behind them instead of in front. It's called the 'Crab Walk.' My sister and I tried it one time when we were at the beach with some friends."

"Old Man Farley was the crabbiest man I ever saw," replied Miz Eudora, "but I never saw him walk like that." She dropped her hands to the floor while Mabel got down on her knees and then tried to push up on her hands.

"'If you get good at this one, Mabel, we'll go to the zoo to see the monkeys. I'll bet they don't have any trouble walking like this." Miz Eudora turned to me. "The zoo. Now that's where we ought to go. Mabel would look real good in one of them monkey cages."

I wasn't too sure about Mabel in the monkey cage, but I decided Miz Eudora would be quite a trip, herself, at the zoo. While I watched the other three ladies struggle to walk on their all fours, I was busy planning a road trip to the beach, with a stop by the North Carolina Zoo in Asheboro. I also vowed to give a stab at the Crab Walk once I was in the sanctity of my own home. *Alone*, I determined.

"Okay, ladies, good work. Now it's time for a break."

"Last one to the brownies, coconut cake and sweet tea is a rotten egg," called Miz Eudora, already halfway to the snack table.

"Surely she jests!" called one of the women from the back row.

Obviously she doesn't know Miz Eudora Rumph, I thought to myself. *She doesn't go visit anyone without taking a little something.* But from the size of the basket she had lugged in, I figured there was more than a little something in it. Sure enough, she had a fresh coconut cake, brownies with walnuts and two gallons of sweet tea. *And I'll bet there's no Splenda sweetener in any of it,* I reasoned.

I watched with a grin as each of the women piled around the table, took a paper plate and plastic fork - also provided by Miz Eudora - and piled on the goodies. While the class was busy working back on the pounds they'd just worked off, I happened to catch Miz Eudora pulling Trish off to a corner of the room.

Before long, they rejoined the group as Trish once again tried to capture the attention of the class, some of whom were already helping themselves to seconds of the food. "Ladies...ladies!" She paused for a moment to allow the women to turn their attention from their forks. "Next week, we're going to be meeting at the Rumph Farm on Downing's Creek Road. Meet here as usual, and we'll take our bus there for 'Fitness in the Field.' Our own Eudora Rumph will be the guest instructor for the day."

They'll be burning then, all right, I mused, giving a quick glance at Mabel, who was already smoldering. I wondered how many of the retired transients of the group would know how to milk a cow, or step around the obstacles of cow pies and chicken droppings on their way to gather eggs. I could hardly wait to see the look on their faces when they got a glimpse of Clyde. And if they thought pulling weeds was tough today, they were in for a rare treat. Wait until they started moving to *Down Yonder* in the "lower forty" and *Orange Blossom Special* in the flowerbeds and hedges.

I watched them shoveling today's treats in their faces. *Yes, they're in for a treat all right*, I realized. *Special-recipe whiskey pecan pie, fried chicken livers and chicken'n'dumplin's. But Miz Eudora will have them so fit in that field that they won't gain an ounce!*

That's how it was that I came to learn that Miz Eudora could make lemonade out of any lemons, even those as mundane as pulling weeds.

FOURTEEN

The Frozen Chosen

"I DIDN'T EVEN know you were here this morning, Miz Eudora," Preacher Jake commented as he shook the familiar parishioner's hand at the back door. "You weren't in your usual pew."

"No, sir, I wasn't," she replied without delay. "I decided I'd check the air and the temperature on the *other* side of the church since it got messed up on *my* side."

"Are you still upset over that air conditioner, Miz Eudora?" the minister asked.

I saw a real concern in his voice, but I gathered it lay as much in the "chewing out" he was "a'fixing to get" as her feelings on the situation.

"I'm not upset," she stated. "I simply don't see any need to go wasting good money when it's the same air it's been for over a century and I didn't see it doing anybody no harm. And mind you, I've been here for a lot of that century!"

"I'm sorry, Miz Eudora, but you have to consider the choir and me. Those robes are hot."

"Then take them off. You preached just fine without a robe for nigh on twenty years. Besides, they've not done a blamed thing to make Mabel sing any better. Why, if anything, she warbles even worse. It's like she's got even more gumption to stand up there and bellow out. P'SHAA! She sounds worse than that old jenny of mine. It's a wonder she hasn't already burst out half the stained glass windows in this place. I'll guarantee you those windows cost a whole lot more than those robes, and they do a whole lot more toward making a body feel worshipful than those robes do. So don't you go blaming anybody but yourself if she goes to blasting out all of them. I'm warning you, they'll be more people than me upset when that goes to happening!"

The minister stifled a belly laugh as he assured her, "I'll see if we can't turn it up a notch next Sunday."

"Turn it up?" she stormed. "It's already cold enough. I'll tell you one thing. I'm not the only church member that's tired of being one of the 'Frozen Chosen.' It's just the rest of them are too plain chicken to tell you."

"No, Miz Eudora," Preacher Jake said in a comforting tone. It was obvious from his voice that he was hoping to settle her enough that she would move along since the rest of the church members were bottlenecked behind her in the aisles, where they stood listening intently to her outburst. "Turning the air conditioner down makes it colder; turning it up makes it warmer."

"Wonder if turning Horace's toes up made him warmer?" Miz Eudora asked in a whisper as she leaned toward the preacher. The recognizable twinkle in her eye replaced her dissatisfaction with the air conditioner and you could tell that she'd "said her piece" and was now ready to go on about her business.

That was until Grover Swicegood, the chair of the Church Council, greeted her as she reached the bottom step. "How do you like the new air conditioner, Miz Eudora? Ain't it fine?" His questions were aimed more at being polite and making conversation with "poor widow" Rumph than his concern over the air conditioner, but he quickly discovered that she was more venomous than a "black widow" spider when it came to that subject.

"A fine waste of good money," she growled

back. "That thing's got it so cold in there, it makes you look forward to the preacher throwing out a little hellfire in his sermon to warm things back up. I'm telling you, if it's that cold in here again, I'm taking things into my own hands and you're all going to be sorry."

I could hardly believe my ears. Had Miz Eudora just dared to threaten the preacher *and* the head of the Church Council?

"Now Miz Eudora," drawled Mr. Swicegood, "you'll get used to it. Just give it a couple of Sundays."

"I done give it three and if that's enough strikes for the Braves, then that's enough strikes for that Kelvinator. Why, I don't even keep the ice box at home that cold!"

She turned back to the minister, with her usual big smile for him, and concluded, "Bye, Preacher Jake. See you next Sunday. And I'm sure glad the sermon today had a little kick to it. Otherwise, we'd of all froze to death." Miz Eudora gave a little giggle. "I'm not quite ready to go and join Horace just yet."

She took a few more steps to where I stood, since I had already moved out of the line of fire. "The Frozen Chosen," she said, snickering between words. "That was a pretty good one, wasn't it?"

My face had to hold its own frozen position for fear of erupting into a horrendous bout of laughter. Several members walked past us, some shaking their heads and some nodding. *Shaking their heads at her brazen ways, and nodding in agreement with what they'd thought but she'd had the nerve to say*, I wagered with myself. It was too bad the church couldn't set up a bookie as a fund raiser, as I heard a few of them also taking odds that there would be a packed house the next Sunday just to see what she "had up her sleeve." I, too, had no idea what Miz Eudora's threat entailed, but I found myself praying for the air conditioner to be running full blast the next week so to see.

THE NEXT SUNDAY, I gathered a few others had prayed that same prayer, for when I arrived at church that morning, "the Kelvinator" was cranked down a few more notches than it had been the week before. Anticipating, *or rather fearing*, what might follow, I chose to sit a few pews back instead of going to the front to join Miz Eudora.

From my vantage point, I had an unobstructed view of Miz Eudora. She was seated on the second pew on the right side of the sanctuary next to the inside aisle, the same spot where she had sat for decades, except for last Sunday's episode.

Church members may have had their ears on Preacher Jake, but their eyes were sure all on that pew. *Or rather the person seated in that pew!* I noted as I glanced around the room. I grimaced, for I was able to see enough of the side of her face to know that she was not happy with the situation.

She wiggled around a few times, trying to warm herself, but it obviously didn't help. The moment that everyone had been waiting for came about a third of the way through the sermon. Miz Eudora stood up, right there from her seat on the second pew, and whipped her dress tail up around her shoulders like a shawl. She then sat back down, as hastily as she'd stood up, her old white cotton petticoat – yellowed from years of use – shining for all behind her to see.

Thank God that was all we had to see! I thought. *And folks were worried about what she "had up her sleeve." Oh, well*, I reasoned, *she warned them. They should have known better than to mess with her. Let's see, she's been a member here* **how** **long** *now? If they haven't learned that by now, they deserve what they got!*

It was a good thing it took a couple of minutes for Preacher Jake to regain his composure, for that's about how long it took the congregation to quiet down after the laughter. Miz Eudora sat there, all cozy in her makeshift wrap, and heard every word of the rest of the sermon. Throughout the remainder of the service, I heard spontaneous giggles seeping out from every corner of the sanctuary. I don't know about everyone else, but it was most difficult for me to concentrate on anything but the audacious act by "poor widow Rumph." I couldn't help but wonder how fine Mr. Grover Swicegood thought his air conditioner was now.

And that idea I'd had the week before about acquiring a bookie as a fundraiser – it still seemed a dandy to me. For I would have bet you money that come the following Sunday, the windows would be open wide and Miz Eudora would reach into her big "pocketbook" and snatch out her trusty little cardboard, handheld fan.

I wondered if Smiley Funeral Parlor had given her a new one when Horace died. I didn't have to wonder long, for at the end of the service, Miz Eudora walked up beside me, pulled a brand new fan from her purse and handed it to me.

"Here, you might be needing this next Sunday. I keep mine tucked inside my Bible so it's handy anytime I get a little warm."

I had to fight the urge to laugh aloud. With all the red faces that flashed hot after her blatant nonverbal statement about the air conditioner, I'm sure there would have been a rush on fans that morning had they been available. Even the coolness of "that newfangled contraption" couldn't touch their rising temperatures.

"It's the new model," she informed me about the fan. "I got a whole handful at the Smiley Funeral Parlor when Horace passed. Wasn't that mighty nice of them? Why, I've got enough fans to do me 'til I go join Horace." She turned the fan where I could see the back of it. "See here? 'Compliments of Smiley Funeral Parlor,'" she read. "Dandiest fans I ever did see."

Her smile was so big that I was instantly reminded of the Smiley boy with the big mouthy grin. I felt a warm smile forming on my own lips as I looked down to see that the "new model" featured a picture of Jesus standing at the bottom of a cliff, a lamb in his arms, with other lambs on the hillside above grazing on the grass. At that moment, I felt myself sheltered in the arms of Jesus, just like that little lamb, through the love of Miz Eudora.

That's how it was that I came to learn that Miz Eudora Rumph was the constant, the variable, by which everything was measured in Smackass Gap, including the temperature in the sanctuary.

FIFTEEN

Doing the Lord's Work

I'LL NEVER FORGET the Monday morning that Miz Eudora arrived at my door bright and early. She was knocking so hard and fast on the front door that I was afraid she was going to jar the screened door right off its hinges. I knew who it was before I ever got to the door because anyone else would have rung the doorbell, or at least pulled the chain for the woodpecker doorknocker I had posted on the door jam.

What can possibly be the matter? I wondered as I approached the door. *It can't be Horace because he's already dead, and there can't be anything wrong with her because she's got too much strength with that "infernal banging," as Mabel calls it.*

She didn't even wait for me to invite her in.

The minute I opened the screen she was over the threshold and into the house. I'd never seen her act so forward. Even for gutsy Miz Eudora, this was way out of character.

"Sadie, you're never going to believe this," she said, panting from the speed with which she'd raced across the road. "God just gave me the most wonderful opportunity. Just flung it right out there in my lap, He did!" She poured herself a cup of coffee before I even had a chance to show my hospitality. "It actually happened last night around seven o'clock. I had just come in from feeding the cows and was getting ready to use that fancy foot soaker you gave me."

Miz Eudora leaned forward, which she was wont to do when she didn't want the whole world to hear her next comment. It didn't matter whether the room was entirely full of people or whether there was one individual behind closed doors, it was simply her habit. A habit I suspected had come with her breeding, like when one of the mountain women would lean over to tell about someone "expectin'." They wanted to be the first to inform the community of that bit of news, but they surely didn't want anyone to hear them spreading the word to more than one person at a time. I suppose I had been in Smackass Gap a good six months before I ever knew what people were "expectin'."

"I was going to treat myself a little like you told me to do with it," she whispered. "Thank goodness I hadn't gotten that thing cranked up before them men tapped on the door. I'm sure they wouldn't have known what to think, me sitting there with my feet bathing in that fancy contraption."

She stood upright again and spoke in her normal voice. "Anyways, they introduced themselves and asked if they might come in a spell. Said they had something they'd like to ask me." Miz Eudora sat down with her coffee at the table in my breakfast nook, with me following her lead. She leaned toward me again, her voice returning to that secretive mode. "I'd have never let them in, it being only an hour 'til dark and all, but I knowed one of them had to be the boy of old man Simms what used to live over on Tusquittee Creek. Land sakes, I never saw a young'un look more like his daddy in my life. I knowed he come from good stock, so I wasn't worried none."

Her fretfulness appeared to calm down a bit, now that she'd gotten past explaining why she'd let two strange men in her home right before dark. She sat straight, poured some cream in her coffee, stirred it and took a sip. "I could hardly wait to tell you all about it this morning. I been up since four o'clock just busting to run over here and tell you what the good Lord called on me to do. Why, it was as plain as if He'd have called me on that telephone of yours!"

A sinking uneasiness swept through me as I wondered if these two strange men, one of whom had "come from good stock," had been con artists and played a scam on Miz Eudora. I'd heard of men taking advantage of widows in the church before. *Church members being the victimizers at that*, I reminded myself. The culprits would prey on the widow's despair at the loss of a loved one, then take her land or possessions, or even their bank roll while the women, most of whom weren't accustomed to doing such business dealings, were not thinking clearly.

While my mind was creating outlandish scenarios, I realized that Miz Eudora was calling my name. "You all right, Sadie?" I finally heard her asking.

"Yes, I'm fine. I was merely thinking of the many ways I'd heard of 'doing the Lord's work,'" I lied, throwing out the first excuse that came to mind while using the same exact words I'd heard from her before.

"Well, come to find out," she informed me, "the two men were there on behalf of their church.

Seems their congregation has been meeting in a vacant building down near Hayesville, but they've outgrown it. They're wanting to build a new sanctuary that would allow them to grow and reach more families. You know, we do have some new people moving into the county."

She nodded. "Just like you. There's some people what wants to come enjoy our cooler weather in the summer and our beautiful views in the fall. Course there's not too many of them brave enough to battle the cold in the winter. They hightail it right back out of here about time for the first snowflake. Just like the birds. They take off in flocks before the cold hits.

"But these fellers want to have a place for their flock to stay all year, and hopefully be joined by all the snowbirds who flock in just for the summer. It sounded like they had some mighty good ideas about reaching out to God's people, so I offered to let them have the five acres there that borders your front yard. That'll give them some road frontage for easy access for all the cars that'll need to be coming in, and a nice place to put up a big sign inviting folks to come."

Miz Eudora took another sip of coffee. "I just can't believe that out of all the places around Smackass Gap, God chose my land."

I still wasn't convinced that it wasn't those two conniving men, and not God, who chose Miz Eudora's land. There was something inside me that questioned whether her land had been their first choice or their last choice. But never mind that, the church was now the owner of five acres of prime property on the road front of Smackass Gap. I decided not to worry, for I knew this woman had been sincere in her gift and that was how God saw it. For those men, and that congregation, their fate – had they done her wrong – lay in God's Hand.

Either way, I wasn't going to let my personal skepticism stand in the way of her happiness. The spirit of giving was bubbling all over her, and I was not going to rob her of that blessing. I suspected this was the most giddy Miz Eudora had been in her entire life.

"I have to go down to the courthouse this morning and get a copy of the deed so I can file for the land transfer."

"Would you like me to take you down there?" I asked.

"Oh, no, but thank you just the same. Those two nice young men are going to come and get me."

Of course they are, I wanted to say aloud, but bit my tongue in trying to stop my cynicism. *Relax, Sadie. You've been watching too many of those cop and detective shows every night. There are still* some *good people in the world and one of them is standing right in front of you.* I smiled at Miz Eudora. *And this whole place is full of them. Otherwise, Leon would have never chosen this land for* your *retirement. He had a plan, too.*

With that realization, I let go of my fears as I reached across the table and took her hand. "I'm grateful for your happiness, Miz Eudora. I'm glad you chose to share your good news with me."

She smiled the largest smile I'd ever seen from her. "It really does feel good to know you're making it possible for others to share the Good News."

I wanted to cry. The faith of this woman was so genuine... so pure and simple, that it made it hard to hold back the tears that came from her act of beauty.

"They're going to plan a groundbreaking ceremony just as soon as the deed is transferred. They've already got the money to get their loan down at the Bank of Hayesville so they can get started right away. The man that looked like old man Simms said he thought it would be only right and proper for me to dig the first shovel of dirt."

I saw what looked like the glint of a tear form

in Miz Eudora's eye.

"I wasn't sure I'd ever miss Horace very much, but I kind of wish he'd be able to be by my side to see what was going on our land. I know this was my family's farm, but he spent many an hour working on it. I believe he'd have been right proud."

"I'm sure he would have," I told her, fighting back tears all the harder. "I'm surely proud of you."

Miz Eudora's winsome moment dissipated into thin air as a smile again covered her face. "I'm going to ask that one young man this morning if he is old man Simms's son. His daddy would be proud of him, too."

I just loved the way she spoke of "old man Simms." It was as if "Old Man" were his first and middle given names. That was a manner of speaking that I'd heard from others around the hills and one that I treasured, for it was a way of connecting the families together. I highly suspected there were also many "kissin' cousins" around these parts, but that was a subject I felt better left unmentioned.

IT WASN'T BUT a few weeks until I unfolded the morning's paper to see Miz Eudora's picture on the front page of the *Clay County Progress*. There she was, in the same colorful outfit that she'd worn to

Horace's funeral, with her head down in serious concentration as she had her right foot atop the shovel, pushing it into the hard earth.

There was no doubt in my mind that this was not the first time she'd put a shovel to this ground. I was sure she had planted many seeds in this land over her years, but with this dig, she was planting a multitude of seeds. Seeds that I prayed would produce good crops, although I was sure that this sower, and the sowers of the church about to be underway on this land, would be like the parable of the sower in the Bible. There would be some seeds that took, some that didn't, and some that took but then died.

As I read the sizable article about Eudora Rumph's gift to society, and again studied the photo, I caught a glimpse of Mabel Jarvis standing on tiptoe trying to be seen between the shoulders of the two men who had made the initial visit to Miz Eudora. I also noticed that one of the two men was named Clarence Simms, Junior. *So Miz Eudora was right*, I concluded. *He* was *"old man Simms's boy."*

I took a long look at the picture, trying to assimilate the character of Clarence Simms, Senior, in my mind. For him to be called "old man" by Miz Eudora, I took it he'd be at least 10 years older than her. I wondered if he were still alive. She'd never made mention of that, but since he wasn't in the picture I figured he was either dead or close to it.

"My husband, John G., would have been so proud that a church is going to be built on his property," Mabel was quoted as saying in the article.

His property, my foot! I wanted to scream. I hoped I'd get the chance to remind her that this property had been in the Jarvis family longer than she'd been alive. *And if it had been left up to either John G. or Mabel Jarvis, I'm sure those two men would still be looking for God's chosen land!*

I cut out the article and stuck it to the front of my refrigerator with magnetic clips. It felt good to know and love Smackass Gap's latest celebrity.

IT WAS A little over a year later that I heard the same kind of knocking at my door. For whatever reason, I sensed that this visit also had something to do with that church. I'd watched its progress over the course of the past few months. It was that church, in fact, that brought me closer to God, for each time I saw it, I still uttered a prayer that they had not taken advantage of Miz Eudora Rumph. I'd heard the expression "they'd have hell to pay," and I knew in this case, that would be so were there anything not totally sincere about their purpose. I also knew they'd get a piece of my mind for mistreating such a dear, sweet soul. And I shuttered to think of what wrath they'd get from Miz Eudora if they were anything but "above board" in their role as "fishers of men."

This morning's visit was not quite as early as the one before had been, but the purposeful knocking on the door was the same. I opened it to see Miz Eudora standing there with an envelope in hand.

"Take a look at this," she said proudly, holding out the crisp, white envelope.

I opened it and pulled out a neatly done script invitation printed on white vellum, which matched the envelope, and read.

The congregation of
The Church of Common Ground
cordially invites you to be
our guest of honor
at our first service
inside our new sanctuary
Sunday, November 30, 2006
9:30 AM

*There will be a catered luncheon
following in the fellowship hall.*

"This is quite nice, Miz Eudora. You must be very proud."

"Yes, ma'am, I am. I ain't never seen such a fancy invitation before. This is nicer than any Christmas card I ever got."

I felt the warm glow of a smile inside, for it dawned on me that Miz Eudora had never received such special recognition before. This probably was, indeed, the first time she'd ever been treated with dignity and respect in her life. No longer than I'd known Horace, it had been clear that it was not his custom to offer her any special treatment. All the apprehension I'd felt prior to this moment vanished as I shared in her pride. She truly **had** done the Lord's work and was being rewarded for it. However, a plan was brewing in the back of my mind to pay a little visit to those two men who had planted this seed of opportunity in Miz Eudora's path. I had an idea that would really be a worthy reward for the gift she had so freely given.

"Would you go with me to the service?" asked Miz Eudora with what sounded like a bit of apprehension that I might not accept her offer.

"Nothing would give me more pleasure than

to go with you to that service." I hastily answered. "And I'll bet Mabel will want to come, too," I added.

"Land sakes!" she exclaimed. "Wild horses couldn't keep her away on that day."

I looked at Miz Eudora's face and thought immediately of the time I first met her. The image I'd had of her coming around Chunky Gal Mountain with a team of six horses, *or mules*, came into view. Too bad those six horses weren't for hire at the Chunky Gal Riding Stables, or that they weren't wild enough to carry Mrs. Mabel Jarvis right on over the mountain to Hiawassee, Georgia on that day. *It would certainly fare better for everyone else*, I smirked.

My mind cheerfully thought of the rest of my vision from that day as I was sure that we'd "all have chicken'n'dumplings" in the fellowship hall following that service, no doubt catered by one of the local cooks.

As soon as Miz Eudora had time to get back across the road, I picked up the phone directory and hunted for the number of Clarence Simms. I hoped I might discover whether his father was still alive, but there were several Simms' listed in the phonebook, most of them with initials instead of given names.

I called three houses before I reached the one of Clarence Simms, Junior. "Why, yes, he is home. He's just coming in for lunch. Let me call him for you," I heard from the other end of the phone line. Within minutes, I had arranged for a meeting with him at his home later that afternoon.

"PLEASE ALLOW ME to introduce myself, Mr. Simms." It was difficult for me not to address the man seated in front of me as "Old Man Simms" given the fact that he was a good deal older than myself. As I looked at him, I began to picture his father as a very old man. At least my quandary about whether his father was alive was no longer an issue. Now I understood why Miz Eudora had called him that. He really *was* old to her.

I immediately saw a charm and charisma about this man, although I was relieved that it wasn't all plastered on his face. There was some naturalness about it. But still, I held firm to my skepticism about his right intentions until I knew for sure.

"I'm the neighbor of Eudora Rumph. I haven't lived here long, but in that short time, I've grown quite close to her."

"Oh, you must be Sadie Calloway."

"Yes, I am," I replied, surprised that he knew my identity. *Perhaps you were their next target, had Miz Eudora not been a willing soul*, I reasoned.

"Mrs. Rumph has spoken very highly of you. She has a lot of respect for you, a respect that doesn't come easily for someone not of our area."

I studied "the boy's" face, trying to decide whether he was untrusting of me because I was an outsider, or whether he was accepting of me because someone he obviously respected in turn respected me. "Then maybe you'll understand the depth of admiration I have for her, and the reason for my visit this afternoon."

His raised eyebrows showed his interest in my upcoming words, I noticed, so at least he was not already tuning me out.

"ARE YOU THINKING of attending The Church of Common Ground, Miz Eudora?" I asked as the big day approached. I had wondered if the nearness of the facility, combined with her being a benefactor of the building, would mean a change in her church home.

"Oh no. I'm looking very much forward to going on Sunday, but I'll always be one of Maiden's

Maidens and attend First Church, Smackass. I'm not into church hopping."

"Church hopping?" I repeated. I'd never heard that term, but I could already tell that I liked it immensely. I'd known some "church hoppers" in my lifetime and I'd always wondered if what they needed wasn't a change in themselves rather than a change in the church.

Miz Eudora adjusted her red satin hat so that the wisp of purple boa flopped over her forehead. "I'm so glad you're going with me today, Sadie. It's awfully nice to have someone share in the excitement."

"You've had a lot of excitement to share lately, Miz Eudora, what with the all the attention you've gotten in the community with this new church."

"I didn't do it for the attention. I did it because I agreed that it's important to have a place to come together to do the Lord's work. You know, there is power in numbers." Her winsome smile I had grown to love appeared. "If this had happened in most places, nobody would know anything about it. I'd be a small fish in a large pond."

"Miz Eudora, it wouldn't have mattered whether you were in a small town or a large city. All that matters is that you gave something valuable and necessary for the good of others. You didn't do it for the attention and had you had your way, no one would have said a word about it. However, through your generosity, this church has also gotten a lot of free PR."

"PR?" she asked dubiously. "What's that?"

I laughed, forgetting that even the concept of publicity was foreign to her. "Public relations," I explained. "The church has gotten a lot of publicity through all the articles and interviews with you. They could have never afforded that kind of advertising. Besides," I added, "think of it as God's way of getting the word out to the community that there is a new place about to open where all are welcome. The Church of Common Ground is certainly a new way of worshipping for Clay County."

As I finished that statement, I wondered how many heart attacks might occur in the area today with the introduction of a new style of worship. *Drums, guitars, dancers, __The Message__ translation of the Bible*, I pictured in my mind. *It's going to be quite an experience.*

I laughed again. *Since when has going out with Miz Eudora Rumph not been an experience?* Not only was I sharing this day and "fifteen minutes of fame" with her, I was sharing her new lease on life that had begun the day of Horace's memorial service. But even with all of my reflections, ***and apprehensions***, about what was to come in that morning's worship "experience," I was in no way prepared for what would take place in Smackass Gap within the next couple of hours. Not to mention the next couple of months.

MIZ EUDORA WAS escorted down the center aisle, by an usher who took her arm and led her, to a pew with a ribbon on it. She had been presented an orchid corsage upon her entry into the narthex, and greeted by the entourage of church volunteers who were there to welcome the expected visitors for the day. There were balloons, tote bags of activity pages for young children - complete with a stuffed animal in each, folders with information about all the programs offered during the week for each age group, along with an array of lots of other items to make people aware of the many ways that The Church of Common Ground would be spreading the Lord's work.

"With the help of Mrs. Eudora Rumph's generosity," I noted at the bottom of each of the flyers. It was at that moment when I understood the importance of including her on all of their propaganda. She was a native of Smackass Gap. No matter what people knew or thought of her, she was a constant in the life of Clay County. Her family had laid claims on property here for as long as people, and their ancestors, could remember. The same was true for Horace's family.

If this place has Eudora Rumph's seal of approval on it, then it must be okay, I imagined them saying. That was the thinking of the founding fathers of this congregation, I was sure. *No wonder I didn't have a hard time proving my point about naming the Rumph Fellowship Hall in honor of Miz Eudora. Did I have a hand in sealing her fate should this day go awry?*

For the next few minutes, I sat in silence, oblivious of the buzz of activity around me, as I prayed I had not made a mistake. Miz Eudora had no knowledge of the fellowship hall. It was to be a total surprise to all when the sign over the entranceway to the large multi-purpose hall would be unveiled following the worship service. I flinched in my seat, cringing increasingly with fear as the minutes progressed.

I didn't have long to wait to see my fears unleashed, for at that moment, a driving drum beat began the "horror show," I later called it, that was to follow. Behind that, a CD blared through speakers, giving surround sound to the sanctuary in such loud decibels that I was sure those who weren't already deaf would be by the time the service was over. As voices began to sing on the CD, their words unrecognizable because the music was so loud and bombastic, high school girls ran down the aisle. They were barefooted, wearing tight black or white Capri pants with words inscribed on the rumps of the body-fitting fabric, long knit tunics – each girl fashioned in a different bright color – that didn't cover the words on their rumps, and cut-off gray T-shirts with holes ripped at random on them and long fringes hanging from the short bottoms of the shirts. On their hands were despicably dirty white gloves with the fingers cut out, giving them the appearance of a bunch of rogues from the musical *Oliver* rather than leaders in a worship service.

My ears were so busy trying to adjust for the earsplitting and piercing qualities of the volume, I found it surprising that I could even focus on their attire. But when the girls began to move in a chorus line of what looked like a jazz dance competition, I felt my entire body go limp.

This made the term "far cry" seem startlingly mild when compared to the services I had attended at Atlanta's Peachtree United Methodist Church on the few times I had visited its "upstanding" congregation.

When the music and dance were finally over, a thunderous applause broke loose throughout the sanctuary. I sat in a daze as a humongous movie screen automatically lowered over the front wall of the facility.

"Oh, look," said Miz Eudora, so softly that I could barely hear her over the clapping. "I think we're going to see a moving picture show. I've always wanted to see one of those."

I turned and looked at her in disbelief. *She approves of all this?* I wondered, stupefied.

"And look at that," she added, pointing to the ushers standing at the front of the altar with huge velvet bags that were about to be used to collect the offering. "I'll bet they're going to pass out popcorn to go with the movie."

Boy, is she in for a shock! I shuddered, thinking what she was going to do when she saw those plates pass. But to my shock, she whipped her hand down her dress and pulled out a twenty-spot and placed it in the velvet bag when it came down our row.

"This must be the admission fee," she told me. "I'd have paid a hundred dollars to see a moving picture show."

I was glad she didn't say that too loud, for I feared the usher would have shoved the bag back our way for the other eighty dollars. My conscience was shouting for my scrutiny of the service to stop, and I must admit that I hoped God didn't see my cynicism as sacrilege. At the same time, though, my intuition wasn't sure it was yet comfortable with the position in which The Church of Common Ground had placed their generous benefactor. I decided to "shut up and hear," as Miz Eudora had just told Mabel, by which she really meant, "Be still and know." I could deal with my feelings about the service, and the church's intentions, after the catered meal.

While I came to terms with myself, a video clip began, showing the various periods of progress on the new sanctuary, beginning with Miz Eudora at the groundbreaking. Most of the action showed her house in the background. I wondered whether that was on purpose, to drive in the point that she was totally in favor of this church.

Again, I prayed that her decision to donate the land would not fare badly for her. My answer to the prayer came the moment I said the silent "Amen," for I immediately recalled my reflection from the day she had given the land. It had been given with good intention, and all that mattered was that God saw it that way. I was sure He did.

BY THE TIME the service had concluded and everyone had gathered in the adjoining building for the catered meal, I felt more confident that The Church of Common Ground actually did have good intention, and that God saw it that way, too.

I could hardly contain myself while the minister offered a blessing for the meal "about to be received" and then proceeded to dedicate the multi-purpose room. At the conclusion of the dedication, a canvas was dropped to reveal The Eudora Jarvis Rumph Fellowship Hall. The expression of gratitude on Miz Eudora's face was well worth the trip I had made to Clarence Simms, Junior's house that afternoon several months back, plus the cost of the brass letters, which I had contributed to the cause – unbeknownst to the benefactor. The expression on Mabel's face was pretty spectacular, too, except that she knocked all the flagpoles over when she fainted.

As expected, chicken'n'dumplin's was the chosen entrée for the day. It was served with the largest variety of vegetables I'd ever seen, and an entire table filled with different fruit cobblers, pies and cakes. Every person in attendance at the Grand

Opening, as they termed it, of The Church of Common Ground left with both their souls and their bellies filled. The only thing that could have been better would have been if Miz Eudora had made her special recipe pecan pie.

Needless to say, phone lines buzzed until nightfall, with tongues wagging all over Clay County, the first of which was Mabel's. To hear her tell it, it was "her" family that made such a memorable occasion for the community. Anyone who had any connections with the day, or The Church of Common Ground, knew better, though.

My favorite comment of the day was made by Miz Eudora, herself, on the way home as I walked her back across Highway 64. She turned to me with that winsome glance, which told me that a tidbit of either great wit or great wisdom, or both, was to follow. "Sadie," she said meditatively, "I wasn't too sure about all that music and those strangely-dressed young ladies at the beginning of the service. But as I listened and watched, I simply couldn't imagine Jesus standing there saying, "Don't worship me that way!" So I tolerated it and finally realized that we all give what we have. Maybe that was the best they had to give. If so, then it was all right in my book. Who knows? Maybe one day they'll have some land to donate to a church, too."

That's how it was that I came to understand how completely Miz Eudora saw the world through Christ's eyes.

SIXTEEN

Six Flags Over Jesus

EVERYONE IN CLAY County, as well as half the people in Cherokee and Graham Counties, was glued to the chair in front of his or her television set for the noonday news on WLOS. Those that couldn't get that station found a house that did. It had been announced on the local radio the day before that the Asheville station would be doing a feature on Miz Eudora on this day's broadcast regarding her generous gift to The Church of Common Ground, now that it had celebrated its "Grand Opening" and was well underway with serving the community..

I had never known that churches had Grand Openings. That sounded more commercialized than I wanted to think about for God's House, but then I was relatively new to the faith so I dismissed my own feelings about the matter. Needless to say, Miz

Eudora had lots of supporters pulling for her. Secretly, I wasn't pulling, I was praying; I'd experienced enough during our afternoon chats to know that she was going to say whatever she wanted, which would be exactly what she thought. *It's a good thing there's that few-second delay on live television in case they need to bleep out something she says*, I thought to myself as both Preacher Jake and I took her to the station for the live interview.

This was "not my first rodeo," since I'd been to a couple of stations with Leon on occasions when he'd been interviewed for various shows offering helpful hints on repairing unhealthy relationships. The thought of unhealthy relationships caused me to remember one particular announcer, a man, who was obviously in the midst of his own unhealthy relationship. It had a bearing on the interview when Leon obviously hit a raw nerve within the man. Had my husband not been such an experienced professional, it would have been quite a volatile situation right on the air.

I suddenly said another prayer, asking the "good Lord" to make sure Miz Eudora didn't get an announcer with a bad attitude. There would be no interview about the church, nor her gift, because she'd been chewing up the announcer and spitting him or her on the carpet. *Although, that might help the ratings!* I mused with a small giggle.

As we drove into the WLOS parking lot, Miz Eudora turned to her beloved pastor. "Thank you, Preacher Jake, for taking care of that old Mabel for me. I knew if she was to come, there'd be trouble. I'd have been more nervous than a cat on a hot tin roof, and I'm already nervous enough without having to deal with her, too."

"You're most welcome," he replied in that gentle assuring voice of his. "And you don't need to be one bit nervous. Sadie and I will wait right outside the studio where we'll be able to watch you through the glass door and also see you on the television set they have in a little waiting area there. Remember what I always say from the pulpit. 'If God brought you to it, He'll bring you through it.'"

"That's so nice," she replied. "I really like that saying. You've made me feel better already."

I could hear that the tension in her voice was nearly gone. It amazed me how Preacher Jake calmed her in a way no one else could, but then I'd noticed he had that effect on most everyone in his congregation.

Except Mabel! I thought with a grimace. I felt sure she was still boiling mad from when he'd informed her that she was an uninvited guest on this excursion. He did, however, politely remind her that she was welcome to watch Miz Eudora on television like everyone else. I suspected that she was still standing on her sister-in-law's front porch where she'd arrived, without notice, to tag along.

With that thought, I feared Miz Eudora's house might have burned down by the time we returned, which brought forth another prayer. Spending so much time amidst Miz Eudora and Mabel had certainly made me quite a holy person.

Preacher Jake opened the door of the station for us, me behind Miz Eudora. There was a woman waiting for us the minute we arrived.

"You must be Eudora Rumph," she said with a warm welcome. Before Miz Eudora had time to answer, she added, "I'm afraid they've moved up the interview to give you a couple of extra minutes on the air. Follow me, please."

With that, she whisked the honored guest down the hall. All we could see was a cloud of purple and red dust since she'd insisted that she wear her "fopher" coat and satin hat on television. "This might be the only time in my life I'm ever on television," she'd stated. "I want to make sure I leave a memorable impression."

That had been a mute point, even without the colorful clothes. And with this extra couple of minutes, I felt sure that she would definitely leave *some* sort of impression.

I gathered Preacher Jake had the same reaction. "Thank goodness they got her in there before she had time to get the jitters again," he said. From the way he made the statement, I wasn't sure whether it was directed at me, or at God. Then the minister did something he'd never done before. He took my hand and asked that God would take our strength and pass it to "this dear sweet lady." Once again, I was reminded that he had good, solid connections with the Almighty.

"WHEN THOSE TWO fellers first told me they wanted to build a new church," Miz Eudora began, when the male anchor asked her how the gift came about, "I was right proud to know that my land was going to be a help to the Lord's work. Then when I heard the church was going to put in a skate park, I wasn't too sure I wanted any part of that. I must admit I was ready to ask to have the land back. But after praying over it for a few days, I figured I'd go ahead and get a pair of roller skates and try it out."

She gave a big grin, and a wave, in the direction of the television camera. "I thought that might be right nice, you know. Kind of like that big

Community Center they've got over next to Brasstown for the senior citizens. I was expecting the church to be playing Bingo on Monday nights and having Pinto Bean Suppers on Wednesday nights. Land sakes, I was even planning on offering to bake the cornbread for their bean suppers, using corn meal I'd made myself right here on the farm.

"Shortly after that is when I had to have a real 'come to Jesus meeting' with myself, though." Miz Eudora lowered her head a bit as her voice became more solemn. "I'm rightly ashamed to say this, because the good Lord had to show me the errors of my ways on thinking about what I'm fixing to tell you. But you see, when I heard that church was planning on having a bunch of young'uns in there skateboardin', why I wasn't so sure about what they were going to be doing over there. I feared they were going to have a regular "Six Flags Over Jesus" right here in Clay County and it was going to be all my fault! Why, I just knew Papa was up on that hillside of the First Church Cemetery looking down on that new church and rolling over in his grave! And he did it without the use of a skateboard, too," she informed the announcer.

"'Six flags over Jesus,'" I gasped in horror, causing Preacher Jake to give me a "shush" sign. *Where'd that come from?* I wondered. *There goes the first impression*, I noted, mentally starting a tally page, for I knew with that statement, there would be more to come. *At least two more minutes worth!* I reminded myself.

Her comment opened the door for a whole new slate of questions from the announcer, a point evident from his suddenly glimmering eyes. "Six Flags Over Jesus?" he repeated, ready to increase his ratings.

"Yes, you know," she explained, "Preacher Jake takes our youth down to Atlanta every summer for a day at Six Flags Over Georgia. It's this great big amusement park with roller coasters and water rides and all kinds of stuff for the young'uns to do. Don't you see, since this was going to be a church with an amusement park, I figured as to it's name being "Six Flags Over Jesus." I just knew that if they had a skate park, a roller coaster and a water slide would be next."

My gasps of horror were replaced with bouts of laughter. This time Preacher Jake didn't bother to shush me, as he was too busy trying to get his own self under control. *Impression number two,* I counted, listening closely for the next one.

"You know," she continued, "I wouldn't mind it too much if they'd put in a Ferris wheel, though. I rode one of them one time at the county fair and it was the most fun thing. Why, I could see all over Clay County on it. When it went over the top, I got a real funny feeling inside my stomach. I'd kind of like to see the church have one of them. I could look out and see near about all of my land without having to walk all the way up to Double Knob."

The announcer opened his mouth for another question, but Miz Eudora saved him the effort. "There's a big old slope at the end of Sadie's property, where it joins mine, that would be perfect for a water slide. They wouldn't have to do any grading or nothing. Just hose it down good and them young'uns would go down so fast, they'd be like Mabel, Melba and Milton T. Toast popping out of 'the toaster.'"

I grabbed Preacher Jake's arm in shock. Now I prayed that Mabel was still on the front porch of the Rumph home, for if she'd heard that comment, there really wouldn't be a house left standing. The minister didn't have to say a word because I could tell by the expression on his face that he was in deep conversation with God.

I had to admit she was right, though, for the straight-down drop off my front yard would have been ideal for her revelation of the water and amusement park. *Impression number three*, I said to myself. *That should be the end of the interview since an inning is over after three strikes.* But I saw that the rules of baseball didn't apply here, for the announcer let Miz Eudora rattle on.

"Anyways, after I contemplated them young people coming in each week with their skateboards tucked up under their arms, and then read in the paper where they were planning to go all over the country for events, I decided that maybe a skate park wasn't such a bad idea. They're just going to get the Lord's work done a little faster with their wheels, that's all."

"This is quite a story, Mrs. Rumph," the announcer finally managed. "You must feel extremely proud that your gift is having such an impact on our area."

"I sure am," she said, nodding her head so that she had to readjust her red hat. "I'm just glad they named it The Church of Common Ground. I have a friend, Mrs. Hattie Crow, whose great-grandfather gave the land for a church in Hickory, North Carolina. They named the church after him. Miller Lutheran Church, it is, because his name was Mr. Miller. I don't think the name of our new church would have had as nice a ring to it if they had called it The Rumph Church of Smackass."

The television cameras flew away from the announcer whose face might as well have been smacked dead center with a cream pie. Preacher Jake and I both exhaled a huge sigh of relief that a commercial break ended Miz Eudora's segment. She was whisked out of the studio as hastily as she had been whisked in, as the studio's stagehands prepared for the following guest, whose interview would definitely be anticlimactic compared to hers. I had no idea who or what that guest might be, but I was surely glad I wasn't the one having to follow her. I wondered if there would even be a viewing audience left. They'd probably all be calling their friends and neighbors and gossiping about Six Flags Over Jesus" and The Rumph Church of Smackass.

Oh, well, I told myself, *at least he or she won't get bleeped out every time they tell where they are from!*

There was little conversation on the way home. Miz Eudora basked in her glory as Preacher Jake thumped nervously on the steering wheel, no doubt wondering how he would explain her broadcast at the next ecumenical minister's luncheon. I couldn't comment on anything between being stunned over her perception of the church's name and mentally laughing as I repeated it over and over in my head.

That's how it was that I came to see what a remarkable visionary Miz Eudora Rumph truly was.

SEVENTEEN

Playing Horseshoes

NOTHING WOULD DO but Miz Eudora have dinner one Sunday right after church for the minister of The Church of Common Ground, Brother Terry Jennings, and his new bride, Phoebe. She also invited Preacher Jake so there would be some common ground at the dinner table, too. I was certain she could handle the situation, but I offered my services, a selfish way of getting an invitation to join the group for the best meal I'd get all week.

I was right in my assumption that the spread would be second only to the banquet of food brought in at Horace's "passing." She had fried chicken, roast pork and roast beef and enough vegetables to feed an army.

"It takes a lot of food to do the Lord's work," she informed me when I jokingly asked how many preachers she had invited. "It would be a sin if I let them go home hungry."

I suspected that not only would they not "go home hungry," but that they'd also be eating roast beef sandwiches on Monday for lunch, or "dinner" as it was called in Smackass Gap.

A lovely table was set, over a tablecloth that I suspected had been made from the same flour sack as one of Miz Eudora's dresses. It was soft and limp from the number of washboard scrubbings it had survived, but the gracious hostess had starched it until it hung in place as nicely as had it come from the linen section of a fine department store.

The mish-mash of plates and silverware were pieces that I was sure had been passed down from generations of the Jarvis and Rumph families, lending a warm, homespun beauty unlike I'd ever seen on any table, and certainly not at the country clubs of Atlanta. As I watched Miz Eudora place bowls, none of which matched, of side dishes on the table, I reasoned as how it was too bad that *Southern Living* couldn't get a photo of this spread. It would have been a perfect magazine cover.

What's more, the mood set by the combination of table furnishings gave me an attitude of overwhelming gratefulness for this woman and her many talents. People raved about the importance of "presentation" at a table. Well, this table had presentation, charm *and* good taste.

A knock at the front door, which I answered, signaled the arrival her first guest.

Preacher Jake came in and immediately made himself at home by hanging his suit jacket on the coat rack just inside the front door. After a careful examination of the table, he gave a long whistle. "My goodness, Miz Eudora, you've outdone yourself. How did you have time to come to church and do this, too?"

"Now you know as well as I do, Preacher Jake, that it'd take a lot more than two preachers and a new bride coming to my table to keep me away from church on Sunday morning," she answered with a blush.

"She's right about that," Preacher Jake consented, turning to me. "In all the years I've been here, I've never known her to miss a Sunday. She's always there, rain or shine, sleet or snow. Why, she's even been there on a couple of occasions when I couldn't make it to the church." He laughed and peered at Miz Eudora. "I should just let her preach on the Sundays I'm not there. I'm sure she's done a little preaching in her lifetime. Especially when Horace was still with us."

Miz Eudora snickered. I was really glad she loved her minister so, for if she hadn't, I feared she might do a little preaching on the way out of church every Sunday.

"I'm glad you got here first, Preacher Jake," said Miz Eudora. "You can help make the new preacher and his bride feel welcome. Bless their hearts, here they come to Smackass Gap with no family in the area and just married on top of that, not to mention all Brother Terry's got to do to keep that church going. I felt like a good hot meal was the least I could do."

I failed to mention to her that her most generous gift of five acres for a church had provided the young minister a job, but I saw no need in "stirring up another pot," as she would have called it. Enough pots had been stirred in the Rumph kitchen for one day.

"PREACHER JAKE, WOULD you return thanks for our meal and our new neighbors?" Miz Eudora asked once Brother Terry and Phoebe had arrived and we'd all sat down at the table.

"I'd be happy to," he responded and set to praying.

My mind couldn't concentrate on the blessing

for wondering how many times a minister had responded with a "No!" after being asked to pray. I guess that was a prerequisite that came with being a "man of the cloth." You could just open your mouth and pray, anytime, anywhere.

Suddenly, my mind *and* the prayer were interrupted by musical notes that sounded vaguely familiar to *Stairway to Heaven.*

"What in tarnation is that?" Miz Eudora shot, staring at Phoebe's purse as if it were an alien from outer space.

"I'm sorry," apologized Phoebe. "It's just my cell phone. I guess I forgot to turn it off," she continued as she answered the phone.

"A phone?" quizzed Miz Eudora. "Don't those things just ring anymore?"

"They do if you want them to," explained Brother Terry.

Everyone sat in silence with the food getting cold while Phoebe finished her conversation.

When she finally hung up, Miz Eudora picked right back up where she'd left off. "That thing scared the jumping B-Jezebel out of me!"

"Don't you mean the jumping B-Jesus?" Phoebe asked.

"No, child," answered Miz Eudora pointedly. "Ain't nothing going to scare the Jesus out of me.

You being a preacher's wife, even if you are new at it, ought to know that yourself. You can't let things be scaring the Jesus out of you, especially in that nice church, or you'll not make it past a month."

"If you put it that way, then maybe we should pray that we all get the B-Jezebel scared out of us more often," Preacher Jake offered, trying to ward off one of his parishioner's famous tangents, but not fast enough for me to miss a first-hand glimpse of her doing a little preaching of her own.

"I reckon you got a point there," Miz Eudora conceded. "I don't want to be carrying no temptations around with me. Can you get on with the blessing, Preacher Jake, before we all die from hunger? If both of you preachers pass, there wouldn't be nobody but that nice Pastor Randy Manser over at Maiden's Chapel to do my service, and if Sadie and Phoebe went with us, there wouldn't be nobody left to celebrate our passing except the 'Maiden's Maidens,' and, of course, Pastor Randy's wife, Linda."

Preacher Jake finished the blessing, and platters and bowls began to be passed around the table as though it were an assembly line. I'm not sure anyone had taken three bites before Miz Eudora jumped up from the table and ran off toward the bedroom. No one had time to follow, or ask if she were okay, before she came barreling back down the hallway with a shotgun, which she slung out the front door and immediately began shooting.

The four of us remaining at the table threw our hands over our ears, swallowed what was in our mouths in one fell swoop and ducked for cover.

"That cussed raccoon!" she yelled, letting the screen door slam shut. "He's going to eat up everything in my garden. If I see him out there one more time, he's going to find himself on the front seat of Mabel's Buick. Or better yet, around her neck. She's into wearing fur critters." Miz Eudora gave a cackle as she carried the shotgun back to its hiding place. "That's what I'd for sure call killing two birds with one stone!"

Phoebe scooted her chair a little closer to Brother Terry's while Preacher Jake watched his parishioner's every moment with a stone-cold face. I was sure he'd seen lots of things from her in his tenure at First Church, but today was off to a good start of winning the award for being the All-Time Most Notable.

"Is she always like this?" Brother Terry asked his fellow minister, from across the table, before she returned to her seat.

"Oh, this isn't so bad," Preacher Jake answered with a grin, finding himself enjoying the looks of amazement on the couple. He proceeded to tell the newlyweds about the Sunday Miz Eudora gave her opinion of the "new Kelvinator" as she rejoined us.

The look on Phoebe's face, brought about by his story, was priceless. "Oh, my!" she exclaimed. "If you were that cold," she asked, turning to her hostess, "why didn't your husband just put his coat around your shoulders?"

"Honey…," began Miz Eudora.

I made sure my mouth was empty because there had to be a good answer at the end of that word.

"…he was colder than I was because he was already six feet under."

"Oh…oh…I'm…so…sorry…," stammered Phoebe. She might as well have put her fork back on the table because there was no way she could have ever inserted another bite of food in her mouth after that big foot went in.

"Don't be sorry," said Miz Eudora. "We had a wonderful celebration when he died. I got that pretty new wardrobe that I wore to your church last Sunday for its Grand Opening. You wouldn't believe the looks I've gotten with that purple fopher coat."

That's where you're wrong, Miz Eudora, I

thought. *Everyone at this table would probably believe all the looks, and more, you've gotten from that coat. Not to mention the hat!*

"Besides, it wouldn't have mattered if Horace had still been living. He wasn't much into that cuddling game unless he'd had a good stiff snort."

Brother Terry went into a fierce fit of coughing at that moment, caused by his mouthful of tea going down the wrong way. That was much better than it coming all over the dining room walls, though, or in my direction.

"Besides, it had been so long since he'd put his arm around me that I think he'd forgotten how," Miz Eudora continued.

Preacher Jake and I glanced at each other, our concern for the new couple obvious in our eyes. Neither of us was sure they were ready for the "winsome ways" of Miz Eudora Rumph.

"How long have you two been married?" Miz Eudora asked them.

"Only two months," answered Brother Terry when he was finally able to speak. He looked longingly at his wife with an expression that I vaguely recognized, and one I wondered if Miz Eudora remembered at all.

"Yes," added Phoebe, blushing slightly. "We went to the Poconos in Pennsylvania on our honeymoon. It was so much fun! They had all kinds of planned activities and games. We played horseshoes so well that we won the horseshoe tournament while we were there. They even gave us a big trophy to bring home, which we placed on the mantel."

"P'SHAA!" exclaimed Miz Eudora. "They didn't call it playing horseshoes when I got married. Why, I don't care if they were Yankees, they ought to have known what to call it." She shook her head in disbelief. "Horseshoes, I reckon!"

Phoebe's innocent blush turned into blood-red embarrassment as she wiped her mouth nervously.

"But then, getting a trophy for it. That's pretty remarkable, right there," Miz Eudora added. "You ought to put it on your bedroom dresser instead of your mantle, though. You know, in case you ever forget how to play horseshoes."

I gave Preacher Jake a "Do something, quick!" glare.

"You did make one of those famous pecan pies for dessert, didn't you, Miz Eudora?" he asked, in response to my visual plea for help.

"No," she answered, taking the bait as both Preacher Jake and I breathed a sigh of relief. "I made banana pudding in case Brother Terry and

Phoebe didn't like pecan pie. I'll have that the next time."

"Pecan pie?" Brother Terry repeated, raising his eyebrows. "I love pecan pie."

"I've had pecan pie all my life and I've never tasted any as good as Miz Eudora's," Preacher Jake informed him. He turned his attention back to his favorite parishioner. "What is it that you do to make your pie so good?"

"It's a little secret ingredient," she whispered as she leaned over to him. "You've heard of Bourbon Pecan Pie. Well, mine is Sour Mash Pecan Pie. I use only the finest batch Horace ever made. I've still got a couple of jugs down in the cellar next to where I keep the rutabagas. Seems the longer it ages, the better the pies get.

"Why, I still remember the year Horace made that batch. Land sakes, it was a good one, all right! Him and his buddy, Elmore Wheeler, were down at the hardware helping Grover Swicegood put out all the extra stock for Christmas. They didn't come home for supper, so about nine that evening, I trotted down to the hardware to look for them. And you know what them three old cusses was doing? They was all on tricycles, having a race down in the basement around all the boxes and laughing their fool heads off.

"I decided right then and there to find me some of what they was into to have for my pies. That batch has been winning blue ribbons at the county fair for at least eight or nine years."

I figured it would be a miracle if Preacher Jake, not to mention the Jennings, would ever try a piece of her pecan pie after that bold admission. I was surprised the pecans in the pie weren't pickled, but then alcohol did supposedly burn off when it was cooked, leaving only the flavor. If that was the case, though, I speculated about why it didn't all burn off when Horace heated the fire under the still. I "reckoned" I'd be speculating about that for a long time because I wasn't about to question Miz Eudora on that. That was another one of those subjects that would never be mentioned in our afternoon chats.

Brother Jennings took his turn at providing a curve in the conversation by noting her contribution. "Miz Eudora, I want to personally thank you for your kind and generous gift to The Church of Common Ground. That's about the nicest thing I've ever seen anybody do."

"Well, you're just as welcome as you can be," she acknowledged. "It was one of those things that I knew the Lord intended for me to do. Besides, I'll never miss that bit of land. Preachers are always wanting you to lighten your hip pocket in the collection plate. I didn't have much in my hip pocket, but one thing I did have is land in Clay County."

Miz Eudora turned to Phoebe. "At first, I was a little worried when they told me they'd hired a married man for the new preacher," she admitted. "One of the churches down the road has been having a little trouble with their married ministers. Seems the last two they've had were getting a little too 'up close and personal' with a couple of the female laymembers. My friend, Hattie Crow, goes to that church and I suggested she write a letter to their Bishop requesting a minister who had been neutered."

The eyes of all three guests opened wide in shock. I thought that perhaps Preacher Jake might try to interject some other "bait" to throw her off her roll, but I think his tongue was stuck in neutral at the thought of being neutered. I jumped up and rushed to the kitchen to "fetch" the dessert as an escape.

"I had considered," she continued, "telling old man Simms' son when he visited me once that they ought to consider such a preacher for The Church of Common Ground, but I decided the land was enough of a contribution. They didn't need my expertise, too."

Miz Eudora then leaned toward Phoebe and

whispered, just loud enough for all of us to hear, "I believe them two ministers had been pitching a few too many horseshoes."

"Miz Eudora!" scolded Preacher Jake, finally gaining control of his voice again.

"Well, it's the truth, Preacher Jake," she said defensively, her voice back to its normal tone. "If they didn't want nobody talking about it, they should have left their horses in the stable with their shoes on, right where they belonged."

That was too much even for me to handle. Coming out of the kitchen with dessert in hand, I dropped the bowl of banana pudding all over the floor, the antique glass bowl shattering into tiny pieces, which flew in every direction.

Phoebe jumped up from the table. "Here, let me help you," she offered.

I wanted to tell her she'd already helped enough with her comment about winning the horseshoe tournament, but it wasn't her fault that Miz Eudora thought the simple, yet logical, way she did. And there was absolutely nothing wrong with the way Miz Eudora thought. *In fact,* I mused, *it's too bad more of us don't think like her.*

"Don't neither one of you worry about that," said Miz Eudora in a motherly tone. "I'll get that later. We're having way too much at the dinner table to let that stop us." She stood and started in the direction of the pudding on the floor. "It's too bad there ain't been a passing, this is such a good celebration."

Preacher Jake glanced at me, with a look that said he wondered what kind of monster he'd created. I do believe that if he'd had something in his hand, it would have hit the floor, too.

"I was intending on sending a bowl of my banana pudding home with Brother Terry and his bride," continued Miz Eudora. "A little token, you know, so as they wouldn't forget our special dinner together. It's in the canning shed where it would stay cool. Would you mind getting it for me, Sadie?"

"No, not a bit," I answered, glad to again exit the room. At least I was going to get a chance to have a good cackle without causing a scene.

"Besides, I don't think Brother Terry and Phoebe will need any more reminders of this dinner," I said under my breath as I went out the back door. "I doubt there's any chance of them ever forgetting it!"

COMPARED TO WHAT had already gone on, the rest of the dinner sailed by. Brother Terry offered a most gracious thanks on behalf of himself and

Phoebe, at which Preacher Jake took the opportunity to also say his goodbye.

"Oh, before you go," Miz Eudora said, "I did make a little something for you two preachers to take with you. I thought it might add a little inspiration for your sermons while you're working on them tomorrow. Some people think that a preacher only works on Sunday, but I know that the Lord's work happens every day."

In that one statement, Miz Eudora proved that she might be missing the boat in some areas, but in the ones that really mattered, she had it all together. I saw a hint of appreciation appear in the eyes of all three of the guests as their hostess disappeared to the kitchen.

She was back a second later with two items wrapped in wax paper, of which she handed one each to the ministers, and a quart jar of home-canned hominy that she gave to Phoebe.

"Miz Eudora, this smells terrific. What is it?" Brother Terry asked, opening the wax paper and picking up the top slice of bread to have a peek.

"I made you a fresh goose liver sandwich," she answered proudly.

The slice of bread fell abruptly back onto the sandwich as Brother Terry covered his mouth with the hand that had picked up the bread.

Oh Lord, please give me strength, was the prayer you could see plastered on his face. It was clear that he didn't want to hurt the feelings of this kind and well-meaning woman. *And an iron stomach*, I'm sure he added, taking a deep breath while trying to build up the courage to thank her again for all her generosity and hospitality.

"Now all of you go ahead and plan on coming back to the house for dinner next Sunday," insisted Miz Eudora. "I'll be wringing one of the hen's necks on Saturday, so there'll be some good old dumplings and some fried chicken, too." She turned to Phoebe. "And I'll fix some chicken livers especially for you, Missus.

"Ain't that cute?" she asked, turning to me. "The little Missus, that's so sweet. I like having a couple of newlyweds near me. The next thing you know, there might be the pitter-patter of little footsteps going up and down these mountains. I haven't heard the like of that since John G. was a baby."

I couldn't help but notice the cringe on Phoebe's face, although I wasn't sure whether it came from the thought of fresh chicken livers or the pitter-patter of little feet. Neither seemed a very good choice to me, either.

"What's your favorite kind of pie, Brother

Terry? I might even fix up one of them, too," Miz
Eudora offered, a childish twinkle sparkling in her
eye.

It became quickly obvious that this was her
way of showing her affection for others – through
their stomachs.

"Feel blessed," Preacher Jake joked in a blunt
tone. "You do realize that if she doesn't like you,
she spices up the pie with arsenic!"

"Oh, hush up, Preacher Jake!" Miz Eudora
playfully scolded. "You're still just trying to get
even for me trying to stay warm during church that
Sunday."

Phoebe hugged Miz Eudora as they
approached the front door, thanking her again for
the delicious dinner, the hominy and the invitation
for the next Sunday. I was "rightly surprised" that,
given the events of this dinner, she didn't flatly
refuse the offer. But then, considering that this
woman was the benefactor of their job, I guess she
saw better. Whether she was sincere or smart, I
wasn't sure, but she announced that, "Brother Terry
and I will be pleased to have dinner again with you
next Sunday."

Miz Eudora leaned between the newlyweds
and whispered, "You know, it's too bad Horace
didn't know more about playing horseshoes. I think

a trophy would have looked real good up over my fireplace. As it was, though, he'd of never stood a chance at a trophy."

That comment shooed everyone out the door in quick order. The hostess stood on the front steps and waved while I went back to the dining room and began clearing the table. I was grateful that she couldn't see my amused face, or hear the robust laughter trailing down the hallway toward the kitchen as I carried the dishes to the sink. There was one thing that was for certain. I would be right there to help the following Sunday, ready for Round Two!

About the *Southern Living* article, I decided that perhaps I should call a professional video company instead. *America's Funniest Home Videos* would definitely pay better.

That's how it was that I came to learn that you could dress Miz Eudora up in red and purple, but you surely couldn't invite anybody over to her house for dinner.

EIGHTEEN

The Big Bang

I DECIDED THAT July needed to start off with a bang so, on the first day of the month, I picked up Hattie, Mabel and Miz Eudora and off we went to The Fam for a rousing breakfast. Miz Eudora still wasn't too keen on the idea of eating out, for she'd been conditioned for decades to think of that as "out on the farm." I had finally convinced her that The Farm and The Fam were fairly close to the same thing, so she'd quit making such a fuss when we went there. Had it not been for the fact that she had admired Tommy's mother so much, and thought of him as the ideal son, I'm still not sure she'd have given in so easily.

"What are you doing for July 4th?" I asked Hattie after we had placed our orders.

"The same thing I'm doing for July 3rd, I

reckon," she replied without giving the subject any thought.

"Surely you jest!" I told her. "You absolutely *have* to do something special for the Fourth of July. Cook out on the grill, have a picnic, do something." I turned to Miz Eudora. "Why don't you ladies come to my house and I'll fix us an Americana dinner, complete with apple pie?"

"I'm afraid we can't do that," she answered very matter-of-factly. "That's the night of the dam fireworks."

My coffee dribbled down the front of my shirt as Hattie's eyes grew as large as the saucer in which her cup sat. Mabel simply blasted, "Eudora! Really!"

"Yes, really!" exclaimed Miz Eudora, looking dumbfounded that we were all twittering and gasping. "Everybody in Clay County and even some from over in Macon, Graham and Cherokee Counties come over to see them. Why, the radio station in Murphy even plays music to Hayesville's firework show. They have for years. It's the best thing we've got in Smackass Gap next to the Possum Drop at Clay's Corner on New Year's."

Pastor Randy and his wife, Linda, came into the restaurant about that time. "Well, well," he greeted us. "If it isn't my favorite four ladies from

Smackass Gap." He made eye contact with each one of us, a typical personal touch that I'd come to appreciate about him.

"What brings you in from Shooting Creek today?" asked Miz Eudora, like it was on the other side of the world instead of ten minutes away.

"A flat tire," he answered.

"Well, actually the flat tire didn't bring us here, but the need to get the flat tire fixed," explained Linda. "We got here with the spare."

Hattie and I both nodded, indicating we understood that situation as one we'd been in ourselves.

Clarence Simms, who came in and spotted Miz Eudora, made a beeline dash toward our booth. "Look who's here," he said, giving her a big pat on the back.

It was obvious that this was a much-loved woman by a lot of people. I got so caught up in watching the warmth extended to her from others that I forgot my earlier shock until the highly reverent Mr. Simms asked, "Can I expect to see this foursome at the dam fireworks show on the Fourth?"

His question received the same reaction from me as Miz Eudora's comment had moments earlier, only this time with more intensity. It was one thing to hear this saintly woman swear, but "old man

Simms' boy," too! I had to grab a handful of napkins from the dispenser to dab at my shirt. Hattie's mouth gaped wide open, making a good match for her saucer eyes. Even Mabel was speechless this time.

"I wouldn't miss them," Miz Eudora answered for all of us, since she was the only one whose tongue would still wag.

"We'll be in our usual spot," invited Pastor Randy, "if you ladies would like to join us."

"We get there early in the afternoon and just relax and read or something," said Linda. "That way, we can find a spot right on the water's edge. It's always so peaceful. I think it's my favorite day as a resident of Clay County."

"Why don't you bring a cooler and some food and share a picnic with us?" Pastor Randy asked. "We'll be looking for you," He and Linda found a table and left Mr. Simms to carry on the conversation.

"My family usually sits near them," Clarence said. "Right down in front of the dam road."

"Excuse me," I finally interrupted, trying to understand exactly what was going on. "What did you call the fireworks? I was sure I must have misunderstood, but then you used the same adjective to describe the road."

Clarence glared at me. "Oh, you thought...,"

He burst into laughter, causing Miz Eudora and the waitress, who had arrived with our food, to do the same. "I forget you other three aren't from here. I'm sorry for the confusion," he apologized.

"I've been here for ten years now," stated the waitress as she sat down the plates, "so the names of places and the phrases don't seem so foreign to me any longer." She smiled. "Sometimes I forget how it was when I first moved here."

"Here, let me explain," began Clarence. "Some people around here claim that July 4th is a dam night for the entire family. That's because the fireworks are shot off from the dam of Lake Chatuge. It's a most spectacular sight because it's so high up and all the fireworks reflect on the water. Some of the kids go fishing off the dam bridge. There's a road that leads up to the dam, and people line it with their chairs and blankets to get a really good view. Then there are those of us, like the Mansers and me, who like to get a ringside seat by the water's edge so we can be near the food concessions and the band. There's always a good concert before the fireworks show. The band plays up until it starts, and then they play the Murphy radio station over the loud speakers to go with the fireworks."

"We better plan on taking Mabel because that's the closest she'll ever get to being like Jesus," suggested Miz Eudora. "There's so many boats what line up on the water to watch the fireworks that she can walk on water. Yes sirree, she can just take a step from one boat to the other until she gets from the shore to the island out there in Lake Chatuge."

Clarence laughed heartily. "I'll leave you ladies to figure that out, but I'll be looking for you. There's supposed to be some good barbecue this year. Come hungry."

"Well," stated Hattie, "I'm glad we got that cleared up. I wasn't sure what was going on for a little bit and I wasn't too sure I wanted anything to do with that fireworks show."

"It's a humdinger," Miz Eudora went on. "They say if you bring your boat out to the bend at the island, you can see the Hayesville fireworks from one side, and the Hiawassee fireworks on the other side. That's why so many people like to sit on the dam road. They say you can see them all from up there, too."

"That's it," Mabel said frankly. "I want to sit on the dam road. If I'm going to the trouble of going, I want the full Monty."

"The full what?" asked Miz Eudora. "They don't serve that at any of the concession stands."

Mabel rolled her eyes as Sheriff Bonner came in and walked over to our booth, the hot spot of the morning. *When I'd suggested we start the month off with a bang,* I told myself, *this wasn't exactly what I'd had in mind, but it certainly wasn't a disappointment.*

"You ladies be sure and park at Ingle's for the dam fireworks show. We're going to have the shuttle service running again and we'll get you right up to the top of the mountain. I hear it's going to be a real dandy of a show this year."

He went over to talk to Tommy while we finished the rest of our breakfast quietly. *That is, as quietly as you can in the presence of Miz Eudora Rumph and Mabel Toast Jarvis, two live firecrackers!*

That's how it was that I came to learn what a bang the Fourth of July is in Smackass Gap, North Carolina.

NINETEEN

The Best Things in Life Are Free

"I JUST LOVE yard sales," said Hattie, who had planned our Saturday morning that started in Young Harris, Georgia, and would work it's way back to Clay County. She briskly opened her car door so she could beat the rest of our foursome to the tables of treasures. "Let's hurry. I like being the early bird."

Mabel sat, dressed to the nines, stewing in the back seat. "A yard sale? I've never been to a yard sale in my life. Quick, Eudora, get out if you're going to and shut that front door. I don't want anyone to pass us and see me here."

Hattie, Miz Eudora and I scurried across the immaculate yard's wet grass in search of bargains we couldn't live without and left Mabel to fume. Needless to say, not one of our shopping trio left without a purchase.

"Well, let's see what kind of trash you're dragging home," Mabel blurted.

Hattie held up a brown purse. "Look, real Italian leather. It's never been used. See?" she asked, holding it right in Mabel's face. "The price tag is still on it. I think I got the best bargain because I only paid seven dollars for it."

I was glad that Mabel, who was in the back seat beside Hattie, couldn't see the smirk on my face as I glanced in the rearview mirror at her own smirk. The purse was the same label as the one she carried, and I knew she had paid over two hundred dollars more for hers than Hattie had paid. She was fuming a bit more than she had been when we'd left her in the car.

As I watched her quietly seethe, I held up a scarf with one hand. "I got a purple and red scarf. It will go great with any ensemble I want to wear for our next meeting with our Red Hat friends. It wasn't a super bargain, but it sure beats driving all over town hunting for accessories. They also had earrings that matched," I added, laying the scarf back on the seat and holding up the purple-and-red beaded "earbobs."

Miz Eudora sat in silence as Hattie navigated us to our next target of bargains with the classified section, the good sales highlighted, in one hand and the city map in the other.

"Couldn't you find anything, Eudora?" Mabel questioned in her usual condescending tone that she used with her sister-in-law.

"For your information, Mabel, I did buy something." Miz Eudora held up a rather large brass container. "I thought it would look nice at church tomorrow morning because it's my turn to provide the church flowers again. It's tall enough to hold the lilies and snapdragons and gladiolas. I can put a little elbow grease into it and this vase will shine just like it come out of one of them fancy catalogs Sadie gets."

"That is pronounced 'vaze,'" Mabel haughtily corrected. "Can't you tell that from its ornate design?"

"Ooh, let me see that, Eudora," said Hattie. "That's one of the most beautiful finds I've ever seen from a yard sale."

Her comment made Mabel huff, which I suspected was more from jealousy of not getting a treasure than being aggravated over the vase. Hattie was admiring the brass container and purposely holding it in Mabel's face as she carefully examined it, both inside and out.

Suddenly, Hattie gave an unexpected screech that caused me to slam on the brakes so hard that everyone in the car lurched forward. "Whose ashes did you get, Eudora?" she asked with a gasp, now holding the container away from her.

I pulled over to the shoulder of the road, stopped the car and took the container to see for myself. Peering inside it, I discovered that there were indeed ashes. "This is an urn, Miz Eudora, not a vase," I informed her.

"Let me see that thing," demanded Mabel, jerking the urn away from me.

Hattie, inspecting the urn more closely as Mabel held it, found words that were barely visible etched on its base. "In Memory," she read, unable to make out the name and date below those words.

"Good Lord, Eudora!" exclaimed Mabel. "You've done gone and bought somebody's cremation urn. There's a body in there." She shivered in the back seat from the chills that ran up and down her spine, causing Hattie and me to do the same from our seats. "I'm not riding in this car with that thing."

"Oh, why not?" asked Miz Eudora, taking the urn back from her. "The person in this here urn can't hurt you. Besides, they've got as much heart as you do."

"Isn't this illegal?" asked Hattie. "Surely there's a law against selling someone's ashes."

"Where'd you get that, Eudora?" Mabel grilled, sounding like a detective on one of the television's murder mystery shows. "You must have picked up the wrong thing."

"I certainly did not," answered Miz Eudora defensively. "I picked it right up off the same table where Hattie got that purse, walked over to the person taking up the money and paid him the four dollars marked on the thing. See the price right here?" She pointed to a small white sticker that was still on the side of the urn.

"Why don't you just dump them out somewhere?" asked Hattie. "Then you can take the urn home, wash it out and it will be as good as new." She paused for a second. "On second thought, don't wash it out. It might act like fertilizer when you put the flower arrangement for the church in it, and maybe it will last for *two* Sundays."

"You can't dump these ashes out!" blasted Mabel. "We'd have to give the person a decent service of release from their interment and we don't even know who it is. Besides that, we don't know where the person would like their ashes dumped."

"I don't think they'd much care at this point," stated Miz Eudora.

"Ladies, what are you saying?" I reminded them. "We can't do that. These ashes might be someone's beloved grandfather. Or maybe a dear mother."

We were all so engrossed in our current predicament with the urn of ashes that not one of us noticed the North Carolina State Highway Patrolman, who had parked behind us and was now standing beside me, until he knocked on my window.

"Is anything wrong here?" he asked, taking a scrutinizing look into the vehicle as I put the window down.

"There certainly is, Officer," squawked Mabel from the back seat. "There's a dead body in this car and I didn't have a thing to do with it. I want out of here, and I want you to take me home right now." She reached for her door handle.

"Don't touch that!" warned the patrolman. "Nobody move." He reached a hand to his shoulder and called for a back up and the crime lab before opening my door. "Why don't you step out of the car, ma'am?" he directed at me. With one hand on his holster, he glared coldly into the faces of the other three women. "Everyone stay right where you are."

The patrolman led me back to his car. "Those women aren't on the loose from a mental facility, are they?"

"No, sir," I abruptly answered, hoping not to

look amused. "They are my neighbors. I took them out for a morning of yard sales."

"Are you sure that one woman doesn't need help?" he asked.

"Oh, no," I replied, looking over my shoulder at Miz Eudora. "That's Miz Eudora Rumph. She wears that red hat and purple coat practically everywhere we go."

"Not that one," he said. "The one in the back seat that was going on about the body."

"Oh, her. That's Miz Eudora's sister-in-law and they're always going on about something. In this case, it just happened to be a body."

"So there really *is* a body in that car?" His voice was suddenly firm and unyielding.

"Well, yes, I guess you could say that, but,"

He didn't give me time to finish before he hit the button on his radio. "How long until they get here?" His eyes never strayed from mine.

"You're barely over the North Carolina line, ma'am, so I'm going to assume that you transported the body over state lines."

"Yes, sir, we were in Young Harris, Georgia, but,"

Again he stopped me in mid sentence. "How long has the body been in the car?"

"Only since we left Young Harris, but,"

"Was the person dead when you left Young Harris?"

This time I felt no need for explanation. I'd learned that he wanted only "yes" or "no" answers. "Yes, sir," I said quietly. I was stunned to see three other patrol cars and an SUV speeding toward us, their sirens blasting.

The faces on the three women in my car indicated that they weren't far from joining the body in the urn. *Great!* I thought ironically. *Then there will be four bodies. Oh well,* I mused, trying to console myself, *at least the other three wouldn't have been transported across the state line!*

I watched in amazement as a dog came bounding out of one of the cars, a man with the leash close behind it. Men and woman scurried from the other vehicles like a bunch of mice rushing for the same piece of cheese. In no time, cars had backed up in both lanes as far as I could see. The entire road was barricaded, as my car became the crime scene.

One of the women, with a man behind her, helped Hattie, Mabel and Miz Eudora from the car and began to question them while another took fingerprints and another brushed the car for more fingerprints. I wanted to tell them that the deceased no longer had fingerprints, but I simply gazed in silence as they all went about their business of solving a case that wasn't even a case. Everyone seemed to be so concerned with "who dunnit?" that no one had even asked to see the body. *Which isn't even a body!* I thought as I took a long exasperating breath. *Blamed those church flowers. Now look at the mess we're all in.* I shook my head at all the commotion going on around me, fearing that I'd be in worse trouble when they finally discovered that they were looking in vain for something that didn't happen.

People got out of their cars to stare and speculate about what was going on. Within twenty minutes, there must have been hundreds of people congregated around the scene. *Too bad Preacher Jake isn't here to offer a sermon and a prayer. He could probably take up a pretty fair collection from this crowd.* As I continued to watch in dismay, I figured we were about the biggest thing to hit the area since the capture of Eric Robert Rudolph.

Just when I decided that things couldn't get any worse, an official U.S. Tennessee Valley Authority police vehicle rolled up behind the caravan of all the other "protectors of the peace." A man in a dark blue uniform got out of it and walked past me to where my friends were.

"What on earth is going on here, Miz

Eudora?" I heard him ask.

My head jerked toward him. *He knows her?* I wondered. I wasn't sure if that was a good or a bad sign.

"Land sakes, if it isn't little Earl," she said, immediately recognizing him.

Little Earl? I thought, eyeing him. *He looks like he could have played on the same team as Sheriff Bonner as one of the lineman. There's nothing little about him.* Thinking back to the sheriff's comment when he arrived at the Rumph home on the day of Horace's death, I prayed that he was a bit more articulate. Otherwise, I feared we might be in more hot water than we already were.

"Earl," called the highway patrolman who'd first arrived on the scene, as he moved back in the direction of Miz Eudora. "I haven't seen you in a month of Sundays." The two men shook hands. "You know this woman?"

"I sure do," answered Earl. "Why, I've known Miz Eudora since I was knee high to a grasshopper. She can make a mean pecan pie, but what I like best is her stack pie."

Me, too! I wanted to cry out. *If you'll let us go right now, I'll bet she'll go home and make us all one.*

"Seems they have a body in the car," the

patrolman informed Earl.

Earl gave Miz Eudora a wink. "Looks to me like there were three bodies in the car."

"No sir, Earl," corrected Miz Eudora. "There were five bodies. Over there stands Sadie. She's the one who drove us to get the other body, which really isn't a body. It just used to be a body, but now there's not much left of it and what there is left is down in an urn that I thought was a vase when I bought it."

"You bought a body?" Earl asked, not at all confused by her explanation, though the other officers and detectives weren't quite so fortunate.

"No, I wanted the vase to put the church flowers in, but it isn't a vase, it's an urn. And somebody's ashes are down in it. If Hattie hadn't had to go and discover them, we'd be back at Smackass Gap by now. I could have put flowers in here and taken the urn or 'vaze,' or whatever it is, to church tomorrow and the person who's inside it would have had a nice service. Even though Preacher Jake is preaching on "If You Think It's Hot Here" in the morning, and it wouldn't seem much like a proper funeral eulogy, it would be a good message 'cause Preacher Jake always delivers a good message. And the ashes would have been poured out in the church cemetery with the dead flowers once they'd served their purpose."

I could tell that Miz Eudora was extremely nervous, for I'd never heard her speak so many words at one time before. Regardless, you could see the relief on her face that here was a trusted friend that she believed could take care of her.

I would have loved taking a survey of all the onlookers to see how many of them had actually made any sense out of what Miz Eudora said. However, that didn't matter. All that mattered was that here was a man who understood every word.

"Where's the urn now?" Earl asked.

"Right there in the front seat of Sadie's car where I left it," she answered.

All eyes were on Earl as he slowly walked to the car and reached for the urn. He looked inside it and then at Miz Eudora. "Do you know who these belong to?" he asked.

"No." Miz Eudora was as close to tears as I'd ever seen her.

"But here's the address of where she bought the body," offered Hattie, holding up the highlighted classified section.

Earl looked at the other officers. "Why don't I escort these ladies back to Young Harris and see if we can't get this mess cleared up? I'm sure there's a simple explanation for all of this."

After hearing all the story that Miz Eudora had given them a few minutes earlier, I wondered how many of them would believe that. Obviously, though, Earl had a lot more clout than I'd realized, for before long we were back on the road headed toward Young Harris. We were even escorted, via the road's shoulder, in front of all the traffic that blocked the highway.

"Ain't this something?" boasted Miz Eudora. "This is even better than the celebration we had for Horace."

"I don't know who our dearly departed friend is, but I don't know when I've ever had more excitement from a yard sale," remarked Hattie.

Mabel scoffed from the back seat. "No more yard sales for me."

"Good," replied Miz Eudora. "That will make more fun for the rest of us. I can hardly wait until next week."

"I'd wait to see about that," I reminded them. "Did you see the news cameras and the helicopter overhead? We may all be plastered on the television and the newspapers by tomorrow."

"We'll be more famous than the James Gang," Hattie said with an animated laugh.

"Dear Lord, Eudora! If all my Myers Park friends see me, I'll be doomed. Why, I'll be the laughing stock of the country club."

"Relax, Mabel," Miz Eudora said calmly. "If that obituary of John G.'s didn't do you in, ain't nothing going to do you in. Besides, those people are interested in your money, not you."

I heard another big huff from the back seat. Mabel appeared close to exhaustion.

"I hope I get to keep the urn." Eudora's face had a melancholic look on it. "Otherwise, what will I use for the flowers tomorrow at church?"

"Why don't we listen to the radio for a few minutes?" I suggested. "I'm sure we could all use a break from this until we get back to Young Harris."

"Good idea," agreed Mabel. "I've had about all the excitement I can handle for one day." She leaned her head back. "Oh!" I then heard her nervously exclaim.

"What's wrong?" I asked, hoping another stop was unnecessary.

"My fox stole," she murmured, nearly breathless. "It's gone. Someone back there must have stolen it." Mabel sat upright in the back seat as she seemed to experience a revival of energy. "Turn this car around right now," she demanded.

"She can't do that, Mabel," said Hattie. "Mr. Earl's escorting us. You'll simply have to tell him when we get to Young Harris. I'm sure he can have his friends look for the stole."

"Oh," I heard again in an exasperated voice. "Oh, dear. John G. bought that for me on our tenth wedding anniversary. They must find it."

"I'm afraid it's a little too late for that," Miz Eudora stated in a knowing tone. "I saw that police dog dragging it off through the woods back there."

"Oh," Mabel again gasped as she slumped back into the seat.

"Don't worry," Hattie consoled her. "We'll find you another one at a yard sale. Maybe even next Saturday."

"Yes," agreed Miz Eudora. "If I can find someone's body, surely you can find some fox's head. If you get three of them, I'll make you a new purple fox stole, out of the same fabric that was left from my fopher coat."

"Oh," I heard one last time as I saw Mabel faint in the back seat.

MIZ EUDORA WALTZED up the sidewalk, urn under her arm, as casually as if she had been going to Sunday School. When the lady of the house opened the door, Miz Eudora simply asked, "Did you lose somebody?"

"What?" The woman peeked out at the rest

of us, who were staring at her from the car, and took a step back as if she, too, wondered whether we had escaped from the nearest mental facility. She obviously didn't notice Earl's car behind us.

"Did you lose somebody?" Miz Eudora asked again.

The woman turned around and took a worried look into her den where her family was watching a movie. "Dan, both children *are* in there, aren't they?" she asked, keeping a suspicious eye on Miz Eudora.

"Yes, why?" came a puzzled response.

The woman didn't answer him, but turned back to Miz Eudora. "Did you find a child down the street? We have a lot of children in this neighborhood. Maybe I could help you locate the parents."

"No, ma'am. Did you lose somebody?" Miz Eudora tried again. "You know, a family member or a friend?"

A look of confusion was now plastered all over the woman's face. "You mean did someone in my family die?"

"Yes," answered Miz Eudora with a nod of her head, pride written on her face with the hope of making progress.

"A lot of people in my family have died, but

not recently," the woman said, appearing to be in deep thought. "Were you speaking of someone in particular?"

Miz Eudora held up the urn. "I bought this here today and we found some ashes in it. We thought they might belong to you. Or rather, to someone in your family."

The woman at the door swaggered as her feet shifted and she lost her balance. "That's Uncle Lester!" she exclaimed. "You bought Uncle Lester?" she asked in disbelief.

"Well, whoever that young whippersnapper of a person you had helping you with your yard sale sold him to me. I didn't just come here and ask to buy Uncle Lester."

"Oh, my gosh," she replied, apologetically. "I didn't even know he was out there. Someone must have carried him out of the house by mistake."

"Your sign this morning said that was a moving sale," said Miz Eudora. "Perhaps that young man what sold him to me thought it was time for Uncle Lester to be moving on."

"Well, as a matter of fact," the woman admitted, "we have been discussing the dispersion of his ashes. Uncle Lester had never been to Kansas and that's where my husband is being transferred. I think it would be nice if he were actually "laid to rest," be that as it may. At least then his remains could stay close to home." The woman looked at the urn in Miz Eudora's hands. "Do you still want the urn?" she asked.

"I wouldn't have bought it if I didn't want it," blurted Miz Eudora with a "Well, duh!" attitude.

"Do you live near here?" the woman asked.

"Just over the mountain at Smackass Gap," said Miz Eudora, her answer causing a chuckle from the woman.

"That's not too far from Murphy, where Uncle Lester lived his whole life. If it isn't too much of an imposition," the woman began, hesitation in her voice, "would you mind giving Uncle Lester a good home?"

"Honey, I've got the perfect home for this here feller," Miz Eudora said in a whisper as she leaned toward the woman. "He'd make a great companion for my sister-in-law, Mabel, who lives next door to me," she continued as she pointed toward the car. "She's as gone as he is. You know what they say. 'Light's on, but nobody's home.' It's just a little different in her case. Light ain't on, but somebody's home. I think she and Uncle Lester would be good company for each other. Looks like his light ain't on no more, either."

The woman laughed. "I think Uncle Lester

would have a good time being near you. He would have enjoyed knowing you in life."

Miz Eudora threw her head back and cackled in a way I'd never heard from her, even during our best of afternoon chats. "Well, I reckon knowing me in death is better than not knowing me at all! Thank you kindly, ma'am. I'll make sure she takes good care of him." With that she bounced back down the sidewalk and toward the car where we all sat waving at the woman who now stood on the porch waving back.

"You're keeping that thing?" Mabel roared when Eudora opened the car door.

"No, I'm not," Miz Eudora said with a lively laugh. "You are." Before Mabel had time to argue, she continued. "I told you he's as alive as you are. And besides, he'll be a good companion for you. We'll put his ashes in one of Horace's old Mason jars and he'll be pickled forever. Just think, he'll be just like John G. You can do and say anything you want and he won't dare to disagree. Most women would kill for a man like that, and I saved you the bother!"

Mabel couldn't get a word in edgewise as the rest of us erupted in laughter. I started the car and began the drive back toward Smackass Gap as Earl gave us a big wave and headed in the opposite direction.

"Preacher Jake was right," Miz Eudora said, beaming. "Sometimes passing on is a *real* cause for celebration. Pull over at the Hayesville Family Restaurant when we get back to town. Dinner is on me. Uncle Lester is worth every penny of it!" Eudora put the urn with Uncle Lester's ashes in the back seat between Hattie and Mabel and began to sing, "'For he's a jolly good fellow, for he's a jolly good fellow, for he's a jolly good fellow…which nobody can deny.'

"Yes, sirree," she said, giving Hattie and me a wink. "The best kind of man to have. And just think, I didn't have to pay a penny extra for him."

That's how I came to learn that the best things in life are free.

TWENTY

"What's Up?"

"WHAT'S UP?" HATTIE asked as a general question to the group as we walked in the front door of The Fam, the place that had become a favorite meeting place for the monthly gathering of our Red Hatters.

"My blood pressure and my sugar," was Rita's quick and witty reply.

"My stress level is up," admitted Mary Beth.

"Mine isn't just up. It's soaring," lamented Marlene.

"Stress level…what's that?" asked Miz Eudora, her head bobbing back and forth from the woman as if she were watching a tennis match.

The conversation stopped abruptly as all heads turned sharply toward this mountain woman. It seemed they were waiting for her to burst into laughter with the punch line, "Just kidding!" Instead, all they got was a blank stare in return.

Finally, Vickie broke the silence. "Oh, come on, Miz Eudora. You really don't know what stress is?"

"Never heard tell of it in my entire life," she answered.

This time the heads of the others bobbed as they shot looks of disbelief from one person to the other.

"Haven't you ever worried about anything, Miz Eudora?" asked Queen Angelbreeze.

"Worried? Land sakes, no! Papa said worrying was a sin. He and Mama never showed any signs of worry, even when they thought we were going to lose the house to the bank back during the depression. We even lost the last cow we had, but we didn't worry."

Miz Eudora gave a complacent smile so radiant, I'm sure it was totally unlike any manifestation of pleasantness the women had seen before. "I think that was the most fun time I had in my whole life. It was the only time that I remember when Papa spent much time with us young'uns. He'd always spent every single day working on the farm, from before sun up to after sundown. Of course, we were right there working alongside him, except for when I stayed in the kitchen with Mama to help.

"But during those days, there was a peacefulness, a restful feel, about Papa that I'd never seen before. After things began to pick up, he was back at work more than ever before, trying to get back all we had lost."

She heaved a sigh that was followed by an iridescent glow on her face. "You know, folks say the Great Depression was hard times, and believe me, times were hard. I can't even begin to describe how bad and how hard it was for folks, but you know…it was a time of growing together with your family. Ain't never been nothing that brought families closer together.

"All them big rich city folk, maybe that had that stress you're talking about. I heard tell of stories of them jumping off buildings and bridges, and the like. Maybe they was worried about losing everything until they couldn't deal with it anymore. But us poor mountain folk, why, we realized that we was rich in spirit, and when there weren't nothing else, there was still family. We didn't have all them people going off and killing themselves. There wasn't no need. It wasn't too much different from our everyday life."

She smiled again. "Yep, them really were the 'good ole days.'" Her eyes scanned the room, passing on the warmth of her memory to each person, until they came to rest on Mabel. "That was, until John G. came home with Mabel and pronounced he was marrying her. The way Papa jumped up and down, he could have very easily jumped off a building. Only thing, there wasn't one tall enough nearby to put him out of his misery."

"Honestly, Eudora!" shrieked Mabel.

"I am being honest, Mabel," admitted Miz Eudora.

Faint snickers bounced off the walls, for most of the Red Hatters had no doubt that Miz Eudora was indeed being honest, even in her humor. "Honest as homemade sin," was the phrase they'd heard her use at previous meetings. Yet, they'd seen enough of these two women to recognize that the ongoing blasts of repartee between them were their connection. It was the thread that held them together, and it had obviously been woven over a long time. It was also a thread that was only visible to those who saw them, as they were unaware it was even there.

"Have you ever gotten in over your head, Miz Eudora?" Mary Beth asked, hoping her words would make sense.

"Heavens no, child! Smackass Branch was barely deep enough to get your toes wet. We couldn't have gone skinny-dipping if we wanted to because there wasn't enough water to dip anything." Her warm, winsome smile from the reflections of "Memory Lane" was replaced by the vivacious grin the Red Hatters had grown accustomed to when she'd share a funny tale.

Peggy, the sailing expert of the "crew," sought to rephrase the question in a manner that would be understood. "But have you ever gone overboard, Miz Eudora?" Before the question was hardly out of her mouth, she rightly guessed the answer she would get, so she quickly changed gears. "I mean, have you ever gone off and 'bitten more than you could chew,' as a matter of expression?"

"Have you ever taken on so much that you got yourself worked up into a stew?" Rita asked.

"You mean a tizzy," answered Miz Eudora, her response showing that their questions were finally connecting. "City folk get into a stew. We mountain folk work ourselves into a tizzy. But, no, I've never done that either. Mama always taught me to do what I could and be happy with that. If it didn't get done, it wasn't important anyway. Besides, if you worked yourself into a tizzy, it meant you usually had a 'hissy fit' and Papa said that was just as sinful as worrying."

"Now that's quite a philosophy," noted

Marlene.

"Yes, maybe we should all memorize it," suggested Peggy.

"Forget memorizing it," said Hattie. "Let's all put it into practice. I think that should be our project for next year. No stews, no tizzies and no hissy fits. All of us could greatly lower our stress levels."

"That's a great idea," everyone chimed in.

"Do you think it might help my cholesterol, too?" asked Vickie wistfully.

The expression on Miz Eudora's face showed that she was about to spill out another winsome mouthful of wisdom, which was no doubt going to include Mabel.

"My baby brother, John G., went overboard one time," she announced, no emotion in her voice. "Nothing would do but Mabel had to have one of them fancy sports car. She couldn't be content with a Ford or Chevy like the rest of us. No, sirree! She had to get one of them foreign jobs.

"Ain't no telling how much baby brother spent on that contraption. He brought it up here and got the bright notion to 'take it for a spin,' as he called it, over to what's now Clay's Corner one morning. You know, all the men would drive their old pick-up trucks over there and sit around the pot-bellied stove every morning, after their first round of chores, to catch up on the news of the town. Folks around here didn't need newspapers. The men had Tiger's Cash Store and Clay's Corner.

"Anyway, they'd go there every morning to shoot the bull,"

Mary Beth gasped, cutting off Miz Eudora. "Shoot the bull? Oh, no!" She gave another large gasp. "They did that in the general store where everyone went with their kids?"

"Wasn't that rather messy?" Vickie asked.

"Didn't they have an abattoir or something?" inquired Peggy.

The women were shooting questions of disbelief and glances of horror toward Miz Eudora's chair.

It was usually them trying to explain their words and phrases to her, but this time, it was Eudora's turn to explain her colloquialisms to the city girls. "Land sakes, they didn't actually *shoot* the bull. 'Shooting the bull' means all that stuff men talk about when they ain't really got nothing to say. A body don't ever know how much of it's true, and how much of it ain't, and don't none of it amount to a hill of beans. You know, it's the same thing they refer to with women when they call them 'clucking hens' or 'chatter boxes.' It's just that don't sound very manly, so for them, they call it 'shooting the bull.'

Heads, all covered in red, nodded in understanding.

"And to answer your other question," Miz Eudora continued with her explanation, "we didn't need no abattoirs. The men knew how to butcher their own cows and hogs and chickens. And yes, they did it at home, but over away from the family and children. That is, until the boys got old enough to learn how to do it for themselves. And then, of course, we girls did get to ring the necks on the chickens since many times we had to do that while the men folk were out in the fields."

I think she was oblivious to the stares and gasps from the women as their eyes were glued on her and their mouths were dropped open.

Mabel, seeing their reaction, took advantage of her one chance for retaliation in front of their red-hatted friends. "You ought to see Eudora. She can ring the neck of a chicken faster than anyone in Clay County."

"Yep!" beamed Miz Eudora, taking the statement as a great compliment rather than a boisterous criticism. "Us Jarvis's was known for feeding the preachers, so I got to ring lots of necks." She glared over at Mabel. "Too bad John G. never did learn how to ring necks. I know a real good one on a hen he could have rung!"

As usual, Mabel should have kept her mouth shut. It was plain to see that where Miz Eudora was concerned, she would never get the last word. Rather, she was always getting "smacked upside the head" with a good dose of her "come-uppance," as Miz Eudora called it.

"Back to the story about baby brother going overboard," she went on where she'd left off, "he drove that little foreign sports car over to Clay's Corner one morning with the top down. When the men didn't make any noise about it, he began to brag about how it was faster than anything in Clay County.

"Land sakes!" she grunted. "He should have remembered from his growing up years that men folk here didn't care who got there first, as long as they got there.

"But no, he tried to show his come-uppance with that car, demonstrating all them gadgets it had and bragging about how it had bucket seats. He tried to get Horace and some of the others to take a ride in it with him, but they all refused, telling him that 'those seats didn't fit their buckets.'

"Those men sure did give John G. down the country." She paused, seeing as how her audience might not understand. "That means they gave him a hard time. One of them even told him they didn't know why in tarnation he wasted his good money on that thing and another said he'd have thought a feller who grew up in Clay County would have had better sense.

"The better sense would have come if baby brother hadn't married Mabel Toast in the first place, but it was already too late for that, because even as much as Mama didn't like it, she liked splitting up less. She always said, "If you burn your setter, you gotta sit on the blister." Miz Eudora gave a huge guffaw. "Maybe that's why he bought the little car with the plush, cushiony seats. He had a mighty big blister!" She roared in laughter, the Red Hatters following suit, with their heads bobbing up and down in rhythm.

Miz Eudora's eyes fell straight on Mabel. "P'SHAA! It was going to take more than those cushiony seats to get rid of that blister. Poor thing," she added, shaking her head with her eyes now down in reverent pity for her baby brother's misfortune.

Her tone caused the bobble of red hats to ebb as they listened intently for the rest of the story.

"Why, it wasn't even as big as half a car and there wasn't no telling how much money he'd spent on that miniature contraption." Her eyes darted back toward Mabel. "Only because that wife of his wanted to show off all their money." She leaned forward to share what she considered a great secret of truth. "That money didn't do nothing but cause John G. grief," she said softly, as if her sister-in-law couldn't hear her.

"And that car, it didn't have nothing but a little old cloth roof, which didn't work most of the time, because I never saw it on there but once or twice. There weren't but two seats, neither of which was big enough for a body to sit in. And that trunk, why you couldn't even get a quarter of a load of cow manure or cord of firewood in it."

She shook her head again, the compassion for her younger sibling written all over it. "But poor John G., he was so proud of that thing. It was a 'Porch' or something. He spelled it 'P-O-R-S-C-H-E' and told me I never did learn to say it right.

"The bottom line is he didn't get the kind of attention he wanted from the men folk he'd growed up with about that car. But, boy, he sure was finicky about it. That night, he chained it up to our outhouse. Next morning, he went out first thing to check on it. Sure enough, somebody had cut through the chain during the night. And you know what they come and did? They took off with our outhouse!"

Miz Eudora gave a light-hearted chuckle of

remembrance of a fond time. "Horace never did forgive him for that. He really liked that outhouse. But I was thrilled," she boasted with a glimmer in her eye. "We got a new two-seater model, and I was real happy about that. That outhouse was so nice. And it was a lot bigger and a lot less expensive than Horace's little sports car."

She folded her hands in her lap over her red leather pocketbook, signaling that she was through with her story. A thunderous applause ripped through the restaurant. I stole a glance in Mabel's direction to see that she wasn't laughing, nor was she clapping. But her frozen face said she was definitely not intending on adding any more to the story.

Red Hat Nanny took the floor. "Well, well, ladies. That was quite a welcome bit of unannounced entertainment." She was carrying something that resembled a red tree trunk because it was covered in clusters of purple wisteria.

"And helpful advice," stated Queen Angelbreeze, taking her place beside Red Hat Nanny. "Miz Eudora, I think you've given all of us a great remedy for lowering our stress levels."

"And a lot of other things," joked Barbara, causing another round of applause and laughter.

"I just love these meetings," said Peggy. "I

learn so many helpful things."

"And I laugh more than I've ever laughed in my life," added Vickie.

"We all know what they say about that," Queen Angelbreeze said. "Laughter is definitely the best medicine and Miz Eudora, you've given all of us a great gift of it today. I'm sure that all of us have learned a great lesson through your story."

"Thank ya'll," Miz Eudora acknowledged while waving her hand. "Thank ya'll most kindly." She gave that winsome smile that signaled one last tidbit of wisdom. "Just don't ever buy one of them foreign sports cars, and if you do, be sure you don't chain it up to someone else's outhouse. Unless, of course, they're wanting a new model."

"Our door prize today is my latest hat creation," announced Red Hat Nanny, holding the blossoming hat high in the air. "At first, we were going to have a drawing for it. Then Queen Angelbreeze and I decided that whoever had the best bit of health advice to share would be proclaimed the winner." She walked over to where Miz Eudora sat. "Well, Miz Eudora, there's no doubt in anyone's mind that you shared the best tip for staying healthy in many ways today." With that, she removed Miz Eudora's red satin hat with the wisp of purple boa and replaced it with the huge array of wisteria clusters.

I noticed a faint tear develop in Miz Eudora's eye as she placed her hands on the hat and adjusted it to balance properly. "I...I...don't know...what to...say," she stammered. It was the first time I'd ever heard her in that way, including the morning of Horace's death. She gave a gulp, swallowing the rush of appreciative emotion that had consumed her. "I'll wear it with pride and lots of thoughts of all you special ladies. It will be the talk of Smackass Gap."

She looked at Mabel and nodded her head in a queenly fashion. "I'll just be sure not to leave it by anyone's outhouse."

"With that, our meeting is adjourned," announced Queen Angelbreeze. "Time for lunch."

That's how it was that I came to learn that no problem, *nor blister*, is too big to handle.

TWENTY-ONE

Precious Memories

I WASN'T ONE to snoop in Miz Eudora's mail on the occasions when I picked it up from her roadside mailbox on the way to our afternoon chats. This particular afternoon, however, was different when I saw the corner of an envelope peeking out from under a couple of others. I couldn't help but notice it since it had a quilt pattern running vertically down the left side of the envelope.

My heart skipped a beat as I slowly and methodically edged it out from under the other envelopes, barely enough to see if it was from where I thought it might be from. "Paducah, Kentucky," I read aloud from its return address.

My heart skipped another beat. This letter could only mean one thing. Miz Eudora had entered a national "Storytelling Quilt Contest" at the continual coaxing and beckoning of Hattie and me. It had been a contest that would be jointly judged on the unique work displayed on the quilt and the story behind the quilt, or told through its pattern. At the time I heard about the contest, I wasn't sure of my neighbor's fancy quilting expertise, but I was sure her stories could compare to none. That's why I immediately coerced Hattie into helping me talk Miz Eudora into sending in an entry. Looking down at the patchwork print on the corner of that envelope, I was sure this had to be a letter from the Museum of the American Quilter's Society in Paducah, Kentucky announcing the winners. *And the losers*, I reminded myself, trying not to count Miz Eudora's chickens before they hatched.

The contest had been jointly sponsored by the Museum of the American Quilter's Society, where the three quilts that placed the highest would be on display, and the Quilt in a Day Fabric Shop, named such for the famed television show by the same name by Eleanor Burns, which was down the street and around the corner from the museum.

My mind raced back to the day I had driven Miz Eudora into Hayesville to ship her quilt to Paducah. Mabel and Hattie rode with us that afternoon to Chinquapin's, where Rob Tiger helped us box up the quilt and get it ready for his next UPS pick-up. It was one of those days that I couldn't forget if I tried. *Of course,* **every** *day with Miz Eudora is unforgettable*, I reminded myself with a smile as I continued trudging up her driveway, still recounting the events of the day when she'd shipped the quilt.

The four of us prayed for good luck, *and God's blessings*, over it while Rob placed the quilt in a decorative box, one that had held ladies' apparel and was the perfect box for Miz Eudora's quilt, entitled *Precious Memories*, After he sealed it and we watched the UPS man load the box into his truck, we all had a cone of ice cream – Rob, too – at Chinquapin's to celebrate the day.

That had been approximately four months ago. It was one of those things that we pretty much let go, with the box to Paducah, and tried not to think about. In fact, I'd forgotten the exact day for which the winning entries were to be decided upon, but now that the letter was here, I figured it must have occurred within the past week or so.

I said nothing out of the ordinary as I placed the mail on Miz Eudora's kitchen table and reached for our tea glasses in the cabinet. She'd actually gotten to the point that she allowed me to open cabinet doors, and occasionally the "icebox," at her house. It had, in fact, become quite routine for me to go into her canning shed to retrieve items for her. Believe you me, that act alone was a great honor of trust in a mountain woman's eyes! They had been raised in the tradition that you never let company help in the kitchen, or with your housework.

After spooning generous helpings of the peach cobbler she'd made that morning into bowls, she then slathered vanilla ice cream on top and set the bowls onto the tray I'd placed next to the mail.

"What a pretty envelope," she stated, noticing the same corner that had drawn my attention. "I think I'll open this before we go to the front porch." That was uncommon since her mail, which generally consisted of cards and letters, the one bill from the power company that she received monthly and the same junk that the rest of us endured, was saved until after our chats and I had begun my walk back across Highway 64.

I tried to inconspicuously watch, consuming my seconds with busy work of gathering teaspoons and lemon wedges, as she pulled the envelope out from between the other pieces of mail.

"Would you look at this?" she asked, to which I immediately did. "It's a letter from the Quilt in a Day store. I held my breath and said silent prayers as she reached a pointer finger under the lip of the envelope and began to open it. Then she froze in place and glared at me. "Do you think we should call Hattie and Mabel since they were a part of this, too?"

As much as I was dying to know the contents of the envelope, I appreciated the fact that, for the first time since I'd known her, she actually offered to include Mabel in anything. The kind act of including Mabel was usually my job, unless it involved letting Mabel unknowingly weave herself into a comical predicament. The sisters-in-law were a perfect example of a comic team, with one person "setting up the pins" and the other one "knocking them down," Miz Eudora typically on the back end of the play.

Realizing this might be a monumental event, simply because of the request for Mabel's presence, not to mention that she and her quilt might be mentioned on the winning list, I acquiesced, sensing she was right. *Especially since Hattie helped convince her to enter the contest, and Mabel said the prayer over the quilt*, I reasoned.

I headed for the front door to go get them, but was stopped when Miz Eudora called behind me. "Where are you going? We have cobbler and ice cream. The letter will still be here when we finish our afternoon chat. I'll leave it right here on the corner of the counter, and we can open it together after we go find Mabel and Hattie."

I must admit that I agreed with her way of thinking. That is, once I took my first bite of the cobbler.

I CALLED MABEL and Hattie from my house, after a very abbreviated afternoon chat, to alert them that there was a letter from Paducah and that Miz Eudora wanted us all present when she opened it. They were both ready and waiting when we arrived at their houses. Everyone had the forbearance not to mention the quilt, nor the letter, all the way back to the Rumph home.

"Since we prayed over the box that went out of here, I wonder if we could pray over the letter that came back," Miz Eudora requested, once we were all gathered in her kitchen.

It was decided that since Mabel had said the first prayer, Hattie should say this one. I was most grateful that I'd not been chosen since I was still relatively new at this prayer business and wasn't yet comfortable with praying in front of others. As we bowed our heads, I secretly pondered whether the absence of a huge box containing the quilt was an omen, or whether the quilt would be sent by a slower, *and cheaper*, method of travel.

All eyes converged on Miz Eudora the minute Hattie mouthed the "Amen," and from the expressions on each of our faces, it was clear that we were each saying our own continued prayer. The "star" of our show moved her pointer finger slowly up the edge of the envelope's lip. You could see apprehension written all over her face.

"Hurry up, Eudora!" demanded Mabel. "This isn't Christmas. Just rip it open."

"Hush up, Mabel," Miz Eudora retorted. "It's not your letter! Besides, this is the closest I may ever come to winning something besides Horace Buchanan Rumph and bath salts." She smiled. "And that lovely new red hat!"

I masked the urge to laugh at the quilt contest being compared to the church box lunch where'd she'd nabbed her husband. I had to admit that she was definitely right about one thing, though. The stakes were a lot higher, and I couldn't help but wonder whether the benefits wouldn't also be a lot more rewarding. Nevertheless, I was sure that Horace had a great deal to do with the memories that were displayed through the quilt she'd sent.

As was probably this woman who is standing here verbally sparring with her, I realized as I watched the two of them. I now understood why Mabel's presence was necessary. Miz Eudora needed her comic relief partner in case the letter was a letdown; she didn't want her real emotions to show to those closest to her.

She reached in the envelope and pulled out a sheet of paper, on which the same quilted border ran across the top of the page.

"Dear Mrs. Rumph," she read, her voice a bit nervous and shaky. Her anxiousness began to take shape in tiny sweat beads on her forehead. "Thank you for sending your quilt entry, *Precious Memories*. It was one of thousands of submissions from around the country, all of which showed a variety of talent and creative intricacies."

I could sense the big "But...," coming within the next couple of sentences. A quick glance at the faces of Hattie and Mabel told me they, too, felt it coming. I braced myself for how I could provide an uplifting manner of consolation for this dear woman whom I had insisted enter the contest.

"As the rules of the contest stated," Miz Eudora continued to read, "the three highest scoring quilts, ranked by a panel of seven judges, will be displayed in the Museum of the American Quilter's Society during March, the month associated with quilterd. Each winner will also be provided free transportation and entry to the museum in Paducah,

Kentucky. Those winners are…,"

We listened attentively as she called three names, along with their cities and states, none of which was hers.

"The grand prize entry will also hang in the Museum of the American Quilter's Society during March," she went on after taking a big breath, which I wasn't sure whether was so she could keep reading, or to brace herself. "It will then travel to several locations for viewings throughout the United States. The quilter of the grand prize entry will receive free transportation, lodging and meals and entry to the Museum of the American Quilter's Society, for himself or herself, as well as for three friends. They will also vacation on the American Queen Riverboat following the awards ceremony at the museum. In addition, the grand prizewinner will appear on a nationally syndicated broadcast sharing the stories that helped win the contest and showing the quilting techniques used on the winning entry.

"We extend our heartiest congratulations to the winner of this year's contest." Miz Eudora paused and turned the page. The expression on her face never changed as she handed me the letter, causing me to question whether she was totally deflated or awestruck with shock.

I looked down at the paper and screamed. "Mrs. Eudora Rumph of Smackass Gap, North Carolina," I finally managed to announce.

"Let me see that," insisted Mabel, grabbing the letter from my hand.

Hattie jumped as high as she could, trying to get a glimpse of the name of the winner for herself.

"You did it, Miz Eudora!" I yelled, grabbing her in the first hug I ever remembered giving her. "You did it!" I repeated, extending my hug to each of the other two women.

She gave that winsome smile for which she had become quite famous lately. "No, you and Hattie did it. You two made me send that quilt. I'd have never had the courage to do that."

"Miz Eudora Rumph!" I exclaimed in amazement, my voice still quivering with excitement, "you've got every blue ribbon from every kitchen and craft category in Clay County, plus many from the Great Smoky Mountains, hanging on your back porch. The walls of the canning shed are also covered with them. And you mean to stand here and tell me that you didn't have the courage to send in your quilt?"

"This is Clay County, Sadie," she reminded me. "Since you've been here, and since Horace's death, I've seen that there's a whole lot more to that great big world out there. I wasn't sure I was good enough to compete with all them quilters what's been taking lessons for so long. I just did it the way my mother's mother, and her mother before her, did it."

I had highly suspected that all those years of experience passed down from both sides of Miz Eudora's family were worth far more in value than any number of lessons. That had been my hunch when I first suggested that she enter the contest. *A hunch that paid off,* I couldn't resist telling myself as I watched her bask calmly in her glory, which I was sure was still an aftermath of shock.

"Don't forget my prayer, Eudora," Mabel reminded her. "I had a hand in this, too, lest you forget."

"Mabel Toast Jarvis, you didn't have a hand come near this quilt. You said that prayer with your mouth, the only part of your body that's ever worked a day in its life."

Hattie and I tossed each other a big smile, conscious that everything on the Rumph home front was back to normal.

A knock came at the front door.

"I'll get that," Hattie told Miz Eudora. "You go with Sadie to call the quilt museum and find out about all the details. We don't want you to miss out on your trip to Paducah."

Or **your** *trip to Paducah,* I wanted to toss back to her.

It was obvious that we were all immensely enjoying the privileges that were coming with being inside Miz Eudora's "social circle" of sidekicks. *First WLOS,* I thought as I recalled her "Six Flags Over Jesus" interview, *now the nation. At this rate,* I reckoned with myself, *they'll pretty soon be calling her from CNN.*

And all of us will be riding on her coattails, I mused, and then as an added afterthought, *unless she pulls them up because the air conditioning at the television station is too cool!*

"Hello," greeted a man as he followed Hattie into the living room. "I'm here to see Mrs. Eudora Rumph."

"You're seeing about as much of her as you're going to see," responded Miz Eudora, causing me to bite my tongue in my effort to snuff a giggle, her comment making me again think of the pulled-up coattails.

"Ah," he said with an affirmative nod. "From the stories that you sent with the quilt, you must be Eudora."

"How'd you see them stories?" she asked suspiciously.

"I'm with the media, and we were notified of your award. They sent us story samples to include with the feature article we want to run for several of the Smoky Mountain magazines." He reached in his brief case for a business card, which he handed to her. "My name is Alvin Trodwell. I live on Touch-Me-Not Lane in the Knoxville, Tennessee area."

"What brings you from Knoxville to Smackass Gap?" she quizzed him, still not sure about this stranger showing up at her door.

"You do." He offered a congenial smile. "Or rather your quilt does. I'm in the field most of the time, so I wasn't actually in Knoxville today. I was in Murphy doing a story, so they sent me on your way."

"Well, if you're in the field most of the time, how do you have time to write stories?" she continued to interrogate. "Papa never had time to write stories, and neither did Horace." Miz Eudora looked at Mabel. "P'SHAA! Brother John G. wouldn't have either if he'd have stayed in Smackass Gap instead of running off to Charlotte with this…this…,"

"Why don't we all sit on the front porch?" I suggested, trying to keep the onslaught of a catfight out of the headlines.

"Excellent idea!" agreed Hattie. "I'll round up another chair."

"I'll pour some tea and lemonade," I offered.

"Well, if we're going to all that trouble," Miz Eudora said, gathering that she was the only one holding distrust for the writer, "I might as well go and dish up some of that peach cobbler I made this morning."

"Oh, my," commented Mr. Trodwell. "I may have to include that in my article."

"Now don't you go printing my secret recipe," Miz Eudora warned. "I don't want somebody else entering it at the county fair next fall."

I disguised my smirk. *Secret recipe, huh?* Ever since the stunt with Mabel at the Christmas cantata, I often wondered how many of Miz Eudora's secret recipes had a "special ingredient."

The rest of the afternoon was spent in conversation and laughter, with the quilt winner doing most of the conversation, and the rest of us doing most of the laughter. By the time Alvin Trodwell left Smackass Gap, his belly *and* his notebook had been filled to the brim. From the looks of him, I couldn't attest to which he enjoyed the most.

"Drop by to see me anytime you're in the Knoxville area," he invited as he literally bounced down the front steps. "You're welcome anytime. I live three houses down on the left of Touch-Me-Not Lane."

"Touch me not?" Miz Eudora repeated with a laugh as she watched Mr. Trodwell turn right onto Highway 64." She leaned toward us to share that "shush-shush" thought of hers. "I don't think there's much worry of that. Land's sakes, nobody in their right mind would want to touch that fool man."

"Well, someone must have wanted to touch him," said Hattie. "I happen to know that he is married and has three children. I remember seeing a photo of him and his family beside a story he'd done for one of those Smoky Mountain magazines. I pick that magazine up every month at the grocery store and read it from cover to cover. It is very well written."

"Yes, and we all know what they say," Miz Eudora reminded her. "'Love is blind.' And it's a good thing for that poor soul what married him." Miz Eudora gave one of her winsome smiles that always made her eyes twinkle with that pure, simplistic spirit she possessed. "But there ain't a thing wrong with that, for once upon a time, I thought Horace Buchanan Rumph was the most handsome feller I ever saw."

"And I'll bet he thought you were a real

beauty, too, Miz Eudora," I stated, sensing a love between the pair that I'd never heard her speak of before.

Mr. Trodwell's interview about the quilt, her stories and how she came upon the name *Precious Memories* must have put her in a reflective state of mind. I watched in silence as the memories of this woman's past cast a blazon glow on her face unequaled by anything I had witnessed on her in all the time I'd known her. There was a youthful radiance there that hinted at what she might have looked like as an adolescent, a young woman in love, a blossoming flower.

Through the process of her grief, I realized, *she has again become a blossoming flower.* Her new frizzy hair, with the light horizontal stripe running across her forehead, softened her face. The purple "fopher" coat she adored picked up the periwinkle in her eyes, which were also highlighted by her new self-fashioned glasses. The red satin hat made her look years younger, and its wisp of purple boa spoke of her feisty attitude. She was a beautiful specimen of a flower.

Then it dawned on me. Eudora Rumph had been a flower, a blossom of rare beauty, all of her entire life. There were times when she was a stunningly colorful and fragrant specimen, and other times when she was an unruly wild flower among the thorns and stones of nature, but she had never failed to be a gorgeous bloom in God's flower garden of life.

I listened as, entranced by her faraway thoughts, she began to sing.

"Precious memories, unseen angels,
sent from somewhere to my soul
how they linger, ever near me
and the sacred scenes unfold.
Precious memories, how they linger,
how they ever flood me soul..."

She continued to sing, in tones garnished with rich Appalachian dialect and Southern vibrato, as my mind wandered off to its own precious memories. Precious memories, which flooded my own soul, thanks to this unseen angel named Miz Eudora Rumph that God had placed in my life. An angel in whose presence many sacred, *and some not so sacred*, scenes had unfolded.

As I navigated my wandering through all the back crevices of my mind, I realized exactly how much I had "come to learn" because of this woman. The greatest lesson she had taught me was that it was okay to be alone. It was also okay to hurt. And it was definitely okay to have "precious memories." Silent ones at night when I was all alone and verbal ones in the daytime when I was with my friends. And it was okay to laugh at those memories, *and those mistakes*, I hastily reminded myself, for after all, in Miz Eudora's words, "If we can't laugh at ourselves, who are we going to laugh at?"

Laughing at ourselves and our own mistakes and funny episodes, I had experienced, also meant laughing about those of our deceased spouse. I learned that was not irreverent, nor sacrilegious, but therapeutic. It made the memories precious rather than morbid. And most of all, it meant not taking ourselves, or life, too seriously as we walked through each day, reaping *every* blessing from it – those seen and more importantly, those unseen.

Listening to her song and watching that cherubic face, it was no wonder, I realized, that she had been selected as the winner of the quilting contest. The precious memories of her mind were as alive and colorfully vibrant as the pattern on the quilt that she had designed and called *Precious Memories*. Through her artistry and her storytelling, she would be able to unleash many buried "precious memories" in the listeners and viewers of the television show on which she would be featured.

Not to mention that she'll have every

television viewer in the country rolling in laughter with her tales of Smackass Gap! I mused, already howling at the image of her in front of the camera in the new hat she'd won from Red Hat Nanny, getting bleeped out on every few words.

I could hardly wait for the road trip to Paducah, Kentucky. With Hattie Crow, Mabel Toast Jarvis, Miz Eudora and myself, it was guaranteed to be a non-stop roller coaster of hilarity and humor, bump-and-grind style, all the way. We might have to rent a car with one of those "little cloth tops" that we could put down just so her wisteria clusters, arranged artfully by Red Hat Nanny on top of a trash can lid, would fit.

As for the ride on the American Queen, I was already certain that riverboat would never be the same again after a visit from the "real American Queen," Miz Eudora Rumph herself!

That's how it was that I came to learn that my soul was to be filled with scores of future lingering and precious memories, many of them to be made in the presence of Miz Eudora Rumph. And as for the past memories we had already made, ah, I had learned that the gift of living was truly, in itself, *the sweet by and by.*

As for the present, I'd heard the trite cliché, "Bloom where you are planted," on far too many occasions. But watching Miz Eudora Rumph go through her everyday life brought that saying to mind every time I saw her or even thought about her. She was one of God's beautiful flowers and she truly *had* bloomed where she was planted…right "smack dab in the middle" of Smackass Gap.

Smackass Gap…a land that truly is fairer than day…a land where you can truly see afar…a land where the Father's gift of love truly had been bestowed on the congregation, through his beloved child, Eudora Jarvis Rumph.

That's how it was that I came to learn that God had provided me with a delightful mentor, teacher, friend, *and best of all, comedienne!* - Miz Eudora Rumph - for many years to come…

in the sweet by and by.

In The Sweet By and By

There's a land that is fairer than day,
and by faith we can see it afar,
for the Father waits over the way
to prepare us a dwelling place there.

CHORUS: In the sweet by and by,
we shall meet on that beautiful shore;
In the sweet by and by,
we shall meet on that beautiful shore.

We shall sing on that beautiful shore
the melodious songs of the blest,
and our spirits shall sorrow no more,
not a sigh for the blessing of rest.
CHORUS

To our bountiful Father above,
we will offer the tribute of praise
for the glorious gift of his love,
and the blessings that hallow our days.
CHORUS

Sanford F. Bennett

Meet Miz Eudora

Want to see Miz Eudora in person?

She is available for your next event or conference - with or without Mabel - and sometimes appears with The Purple Stallion, singer extraordaire. On rare special occasions, Hattie Crow may even be seen sharing the stage with Miz Eudora!

http://mizeudora.com

RUDY THE RED PIG

Miz Eudora Rumph is not the only "red" character of Catherine Ritch Guess. Through her Rudy the Red Pig children's series, she is the founder of Rudy & Friends Reading Pen, Inc., a non-profit organzation created to promote literacy with children throughout the country, while helping to replenish school (public, private and Christian) libraries destroyed by natural disasters.

Rudy, now a year old, has collected over 10,000 new books for children, has his own Bookmobile and Book Trough and has traveled to 28 states to spark, inspire and movitate creativity in children while reading to them. With the help of many volunteers, most of them from St. Johns Lutheran Church in Concord, NC, he provided a free cultural arts camp - Rudy's Great Gulf Adventures - designed to socially and emotionally "rebuild" the lives of children affected by Hurricane Katrina. This will be an ongoing project for any devastated area of the country.

http://rudytheredpig.com

ABOUT THE AUTHOR

Catherine Ritch Guess is the author of eighteen books, all of the inspirational genre, which include fiction, non-fiction and children's titles. In addition, she is a published composer and a frequent speaker/musician for a wide range of conferences and events.

She is currently working on two new children's books, *This Land is Whose Land?* - a non-fiction on eminent domain, and four novels, one of which is *Precious Memories,* the next volume in The Winsome Ways of Miz Eudora Rumph.

Her most treasured activity is spending time with her family at home in North Carolina.

www.ciridmus.com